AMERICAN PASSENGER TRAINS

WWII to AMTRAK

Patrick C. Dorin

Iconografix

Iconografix
PO Box 446
Hudson, Wisconsin 54016 USA

Library of Congress Control Number: 2008944048

ISBN-13: 978-1-58388-232-0
ISBN-10: 1-58388-232-4

09 10 11 12 13 14 6 5 4 3 2 1

Printed in China

Cover and book design by Dan Perry

Copyedited by Andy Lindberg

Cover Photos by Herman Page

BOOK PROPOSALS

Iconografix is a publishing company specializing in books for transportation enthusiasts. We publish in a number of different areas, including Automobiles, Auto Racing, Buses, Construction Equipment, Emergency Equipment, Farming Equipment, Railroads & Trucks. The Iconografix imprint is constantly growing and expanding into new subject areas.

Authors, editors, and knowledgeable enthusiasts in the field of transportation history are invited to contact the Editorial Department at Iconografix, Inc., PO Box 446, Hudson, WI 54016.

www.iconografixinc.com

DEDICATED TO THE MEMORY OF DENNIS MCGUIRE

Chair of the Class Reunion Committees

And longtime classmate and friend at Emerson High School in Gary, Indiana

AND TO HIGH SCHOOL REUNION COMMITTEE MEMBERS

Who Have Played a Major Role in Keeping the Classmates

Connected with One Another for Many Years

ACKNOWLEDGEMENTS

Many photographers and researchers provided superb assistance with information and photos for this overview of North American rail passenger services from the 1940s to the Amtrak Era. The author wishes to thank the following people for their wisdom and the photos for use in the book.

W. C. Whittaker, Anna Whittaker, Sy Dykhouse, Jim Scribbins, Harold K. Vollrath, William S. Kuba, Jay Williams, Wayne Olsen, Jim Harris, Michael L. McBride, Bob Lorenz, Herman Page, Thomas A. Dorin, Michael A. Dorin, Frank Schnick, Jeff Koeller, Jr., Dale Holm, Lloyd Keyser, Mark Llanuza, Dan Mackey, William A. Raia, Cliff Black with Amtrak, and Michele Pearson with the Lake Superior Railroad Museum in Duluth, Minnesota. Should any name have been missed, this writer apologizes and trusts it will be found in the appropriate location in the book.

Again, thank you to each and everyone for your kind assistance for this new book.

TABLE OF CONTENTS

INTRODUCTION

The purpose of this book is to provide an overview of the passenger train services from the 1940s to the Amtrak Era beginning in 1971. The 1940s and '50s era of rail passenger service in North America was a period of time with many new streamliners. It was a transition period from steam to diesel power and from heavyweight passenger equipment to the new streamlined cars. Many trains operated with a mixture of equipment consisting of the heavyweight cars dating from 1920s and the new streamlined cars. It was a period of change, with periods of passenger traffic growth on many routes and then a decline that nearly spelled the end of train service in North America. This in turn led to the creation of Amtrak, which as of 2008 is experiencing substantial growth in passenger traffic with new record levels. The commuter train services are also experiencing such growth. And all of this is happening when there are still many folks in North America who believe that railroads will soon be past history. This not only applies to passenger service but freight service as well. This writer has even heard that it would be easier for the coal mines to simply ship by truck to the power plants. Can you imagine that?

The focus of this book is to review the types of trains operated from the 1940s to the '60s. This includes local runs serving many communities along the route, corridor operations such as between Washington, D. C., and New York City, long distance trains that provided overnight and daytime travel, and the transcontinental services. The following chapters include the variety of train services with photos of trains and equipment, timetables, and other pertinent information about specific operations. It should be noted that there are overlaps in the types of services. For example, local and/or commuter trains making all stops also operated in heavy-duty corridors as well as the branch lines and long distance main line routes.

The book begins with the types of corridor train services in the Northeast, the Midwest and the West Coast. A chapter reviews the local train operations with service to every station along the route. The long distance services include the overnight, the daytime schedules plus Florida travel and the West Coast. The transcontinental service chapters include the routes from the Midwest and South to the West Coast and the Canadian transcontinental services.

Basically, the types of train services are divided, in part, by the mileages for their operations as follows:

Corridor Routes extend from about 75 miles to about 250 miles. One exception with a greater distance is the Toronto – Montreal route with 335 miles and service to a densely populated area.

The local trains generally operated over very short distances, such as a 25-mile branch line, or much longer routes, such as 500 miles. However, one can find locals that covered even longer distances.

The long distance trains cover routes from about 300 miles to as much as 1800 miles. Train services include the "Overnight – Everynight" runs, as well as the daytime schedules. Transcontinental trains basically cover routes extending from the East and Midwest all the way to the Pacific Coast. Route mileages for these operations were (and are) well over 2000 miles, whether the run is from New Orleans, Chicago, or St. Louis. Through cars were operated from New York City and Washington, D. C., to the West Coast.

There is much to learn from the mid-20th Century in terms of how train services provided a convenient service for many communities. It is interesting to note that there were many railroad lines, such as the Chicago and North Western to Northern Michigan and Wisconsin that had as many as three long distance trains a day in each direction, plus freight services. And now many of those railroad lines are gone. In fact, much of northern Wisconsin, Michigan and Minnesota do not even have bus services, let alone a railroad line that could eventually provide service. However, that is a subject for seminars, transportation classes, and perhaps another book – *The Need for Revitalized Rail Service*.

It is our hope that the readers will find this book informative with new knowledge levels regarding passenger train service, not only for the enjoyment of looking at history; but also for the possibility of creating new passenger train services in North America for reducing energy needs, traffic congestion, and pollution, improving travel safety, as well as enhancing the art of model railroading.

Best wishes and happy railroading,
Patrick C. Dorin
Superior, Wisconsin
October 2008

The Duluth-Superior and the Twin Cities corridor, a distance of 160 miles, had five trains daily in each direction during the 1950s. Three railroads, the Great Northern, Northern Pacific and the Soo Line operated a pool service with coordinated schedules with a ticket system good on all three lines. The NP operated two trains each way with one being an overnight, the Soo operated one train, while the GN operated two trains each way. This photo by Wayne C. Olsen shows the GN's Gopher arriving in Duluth with a six-car consist including a parlor lounge as the last car. The GN's Gopher schedule covered the 160 miles in three hours, fifteen minutes.

CHAPTER 1

CORRIDOR and SHORT DISTANCE PASSENGER SERVICE

The purpose of this chapter is to review some of the heavy corridor passenger services, such as New York City and Philadelphia, as well as the some of the shorter distance operations. The distance mileage for this group is 250 miles or less. Corridor routes are generally defined as heavily populated areas, which would describe the Northeast corridor, and other routes such as Chicago and Milwaukee. Perhaps an exception to the mileage would be the heavily populated corridor between Montreal and Toronto, which is 335 miles. Some of the shorter distance train operations that served major cities, but operated through rural areas, are also included in this chapter. One example would be the Monon's Chicago – Indianapolis route of 183 miles.

There were a number of corridor routes developed in North America since railroad passenger service began prior to the 1850s. Basically the corridor services were operated between metropolitan areas, such as New York – Boston, and generally provided several trains in each direction on a daily basis. The daily service levels varied from as much as a train every 30 minutes or an hour to as few as five trains in each direction. The corridor routes also included long distance trains. Reviewing the time period from the late 1940s through the 1960s, there were several routes across the continent. The following is a partial list of the corridor services in North America for the time period described in this book:

One could consider a number of other routes as

This view shows the Gopher departing the Duluth Union Depot at 4:30 p.m. with a six-car consist for Minneapolis and St. Paul. The Duluth depot (still in existence in 2008 as a museum and a train station.) is in the background. There were also two other depots. Te Soo Line was to the left but is not visible, and still another depot for the Chicago and North Western was located a block east of the Duluth Union Depot and is obviously not visible in this photo. Thus Duluth once had three downtown stations. As a sidebar, the C&NW (through its subsidiary known as the Omaha) once operated two trains each way to the Twin Cities, while the Soo, NP, and the GN once operated three trains each way. *Wayne C. Olsen*

Route	Mileage	Railroad
New York City – Philadelphia	91	Pennsylvania
New York City – Washington, D.C.	226	Pennsylvania
New York City – Boston	230	New Haven
Chicago – Milwaukee Chicago – Green Bay	85 200	The Milwaukee Road Chicago and North Western Chicago, North Shore and Milwaukee (Electric Line to Milwaukee)
St. Paul – Minneapolis – Duluth (Pool Service)	160	Northern Pacific Great Northern Soo Line
Seattle – Portland (Pool Service)	186	Great Northern Northern Pacific Union Pacific
Seattle – Vancouver, BC	157	Great Northern
Los Angeles – San Diego	128	Santa Fe
Montreal – Toronto	335	Canadian National Canadian Pacific
Montreal – Quebec City (Pool Service)	178	Canadian National Canadian Pacific
San Francisco/Oakland – Sacramento	92	Southern Pacific

One of the West Coast corridors was the San Francisco-Oakland and Sacramento route on the Southern Pacific. The SP had several long distance trains over the route as well as trains for the territory, such as No. 246 shown here departing the Oakland Pier for Sacramento on November 11, 1947. It is interesting to note that now, in 2008, Amtrak California operates 16 trains in each direction between Oakland and Sacramento compared to approximately 10 each way in 1951 depending upon the day of the week and intermediate terminals. The 1951 count does not include long distance trains, such as the San Francisco Overland and others. The Amtrak count does not include long distance trains either. *W. C. Whittaker*

corridor systems, such as New York City – Albany on the New York Central, Chicago – Indianapolis on the Monon Railroad and Chicago – Grand Rapids, Michigan, and Grand Rapids – Detroit on the Chesapeake and Ohio/Pere Marquette. Many of the other routes were generally handled by the longer distance train services. With the exception of a few RDC runs, known as the Beeliner on the NYC, all of the Albany services were handled by through trains. Regarding the Monon Railroad, the company once operated two daily trains in each direction between the two cities. The route was basically considered a longer distance type of service, but as we move deeper into the 21st century, Chicago – Indianapolis is but one example of the need for new levels of corridor services.

The heaviest corridor routes were between Boston and Washington on the New Haven and the Pennsylvania Railroads. The routes supported numerous trains between terminals, plus additional trains the entire distance between Boston and Washington, D.C. All of the trains provided coach seating plus parlor car and food and beverage service on many of

the longer distance trains, i.e., New York – Washington, and New York – Boston. The overnight trains also included sleeping car service.

The New Haven, by the way, once earned a profit on its food and beverage service. This is a piece of research that needs to be done to benefit such services in the 21st century.

The Midwest and West Coast services were not as frequent as the routes in the East. However, as one well knows, the population densities on the West Coast were not even close to the levels as they now exist in the 21st century. Nevertheless, the train services were convenient with some rather interesting innovations.

One of the highest frequencies of service could be found between Chicago and Milwaukee. The corridor had three railroads, the Milwaukee Road, the Chicago and North Western and the Chicago, North Shore and Milwaukee. The latter was an interurban line, with smaller and lighter electric passenger equipment. The North Shore never did invest in commuter electric passenger equipment, such as

A low-density corridor on the Chesapeake and Ohio was the route between Grand Rapids and Detroit, Michigan, a distance of 153 miles. In 1969, there were three trains in each direction on weekdays. Saturday and Sunday had two trains each way. Patronage had dropped over the years and two-car consists were common. Trains 11 and 14 were the morning trains while No. 12 and 15 were daily afternoon trains and covered the route in 3 hours and 15 minutes on weekends. The C&O Detroit – Grand Rapids train services were known as the Pere Marquettes. Train No. 14 is shown here ready to depart Grand Rapids with the usual two-car consist. The two-car trains fall into the category for model railroaders as "Model Railroad Pike Size Trains." *Sy Dykhouse, October 1969*

the Chicago, South Shore and South Bend. This was a bit of a drawback for handling passengers over longer distances, but it was a basic requirement since the North Shore operated over the CTA's "L" System in downtown Chicago. Between the three railroads, the service levels between Chicago and Milwaukee was frequent with well over 40 trains per day in each direction.

The Milwaukee Road and C&NW services included the long distance trains. Parlor car seating and food and beverage services were provided by both railroads on several trains. The North Shore also had food and beverage service on its Electroliners.

The St. Paul to Duluth passenger service, also know as the Twin Cities – Twin Ports services with Minneapolis and Superior, Wisconsin, as part of the respective metropolitan areas, once had 11 trains in each direction. There were three each way on the Soo, Great Northern, and Northern Pacific; and two each way on the Omaha, a subsidiary of the Chicago and North Western. By the 1930s, the Omaha services were gone.

During the 1930s, the other three railroads worked out pool agreements where train tickets could be used on any of the three routes. The train services were reduced to an overnight train and a day schedule on

the NP, a morning and afternoon schedule in each direction on the GN, and a noontime schedule in each direction on the Soo Line.

The NP provided sleeping car service on the overnight train, which also handled mail and express. The GN provided both coach and parlor car service on its pair of trains. The morning Badger was basically a local train, while the afternoon Gopher was on a faster schedule. The noon schedule for the Soo Line was a local train with one head-end car and one or two coaches. It fit the local train image nicely with a 4-6-2 Pacific during the days of steam, and GP-9 upon dieselization.

Moving out west, the Great Northern operated a minimum of three trains a day in each direction between Seattle and Vancouver. The trains provided food and beverage service and parlor car seating. The streamlined trains were known as the Internationals. The GN also operated a local train over the route for a fourth train in each direction.

The Seattle – Portland route was also a pool service with the Union Pacific, Northern Pacific and the Great Northern. During the 1940s and '50s, there were four trains in each direction. The agreement for the pool service included trading the fourth train among the three railroads on a time cycle. Thus, the GN would have two each way, and then the NP and so on to the UP. The various services levels dwindled substantially as time moved on with the loss of the fourth train schedule.

The populated area of southern California between Los Angeles and San Diego was handled by the Santa Fe. During the mid-1950s, the Santa Fe operated six trains in each direction, of which five were known as the San Diegans. By the mid-1960s, this was reduced to three trains in each direction, which was the schedule until Amtrak Day.

It should be noted that the corridor services included schedules with a limited number of stops as well as local trains. Local train services covered a vast area throughout North America, such as populated areas with commuter train services as well as rural areas on both main lines and branch lines. Local trains are part of the next chapter in this review of North American passenger rail services.

Following are photos and timetables of the various types of corridor services in North America including information on equipment and onboard accommodations and other types of service.

Moving into the heavier corridor services, one such route was operated by the Canadian National between Toronto and Windsor, Ontario (Detroit), a distance of just over 228 miles. (This was only part of the total corridor with another route to Sarnia, Ontario, across the border from Port Huron, Michigan.) In 1969, the CN operated trains designated as Tempos and Railiners. The Railiners were equipped with Rail Diesel cars, while the Tempos were equipped with new streamlined equipment. The 1969 schedules illustrate two Tempos to Windsor-Detroit and one Tempo and one Railiner to Sarnia. This photo illustrates CN's No. 145, the "Tempo" arriving at Windsor with a Montreal Locomotive Works 1800 Horsepower road-switcher leading three coaches and one parlor car. *Patrick C. Dorin*

Canadian National parlor car No. 321 rests between assignments at Windsor, Ontario, in September 1971. Not all of the Tempos carried club cars, as the CN called its parlor cars. Interiors had single seating on one side of the aisle and two seats with a wide arm between on the other side, thus increasing the seating capacity by nearly 50%. *Jim Scribbins*

The Montreal – Toronto corridor is 335 miles long. Both the Canadian National and Canadian Pacific operated passenger service with a pool service. As time went on, the CN route was the primary passenger service carrier, which evolved into the VIA Rail Canada train services. In this view, the westbound Bonaventure is moving through Dorval, Quebec, about 12 miles west of Montreal. The Bonaventure was an afternoon train scheduled for 5 hours, 50 minutes to Toronto. Many of the Montreal – Toronto trains provided both coach and parlor car seating as well as food and beverage service, September 20, 1966. *Jim Scribbins, William Raia Collection*

The heaviest corridors in North America were, and still are, in the Northeastern United States. A major section of the New Haven Railroad's Boston – New York City route was electrified, especially for the commuter rail service. However, the long distance trains operated with electric power between New Haven and New York City. This photo illustrates the type of electric power, an EP-4 built by Alco-General Electric in 1938, with a train in electrified territory near New York in 1941. *Harold K. Vollrath Collection*

According to the photo information, this New Haven train is known as the East Wind and is shown here with steam power at New Haven, Connecticut, in April 1940. *Harold K. Vollrath Collection*

A New Haven passenger extra with two coaches is at New Haven with steam power. Note the overhead wires for the electrified territory. *Harold K. Vollrath Collection*

The New Haven operated high level steam power in the New York – Boston corridor, such as 1400, Type I-5 built by Baldwin in 1937. it is shown here leading a 10-car train, including an RPO-Baggage car on the head-end. In the early 1940s, the New Haven operated over 20 trains a day in each direction between New York and Boston. This number varied depending upon the day of the week, and the season of the year. There were a number of trains that operated only one day per week. One example was the Seashore Express, which was a Monday-only train from Boston to New York. *Harold K. Vollrath Collection*

Another example of New Haven steam power in passenger service was a group of 4-8-2s, such as the 1380 shown here in service at Yarmouth, Massachusetts. *Harold K. Vollrath Collection*

It is August 7, 1956 and the New Haven's train No. 75 is rolling through the Bronx at New York City. The visible consist is a string of heavyweight coaches. This particular segment of track is equipped for third-rail electric power. The New Haven motive power was equipped for both overhead wire and third-rail systems. *William Raia*

New Haven's train No. 8, the Ambassador, with streamlined equipment is picking up speed in the overhead wire territory near New Rochelle, New York, in July 1957. *William Raia*

New Haven electric power in the new color scheme is heading up an eleven-car train, including coaches, parlor car and food and beverage equipment. The train is in third-rail territory, but note the pantographs on top of the 371. This November 1958 photo shows the type of third rail at New York City. *William Raia*

The Pennsylvania Railroad operated a high frequency of trains between New York City, Philadelphia and Washington, D. C., throughout the day right up to the Amtrak debut in May 1971. Many of the trains were powered by the famous electric power, the GG-1, such as the 4822 shown here at Baltimore in April 1949. *William S. Kuba*

The PRR Congressionals and the Senators were equipped with corrugated side equipment built by the Budd Company with the silver color scheme. The PRR's 4877 is leading one of the Budd-built trains through Harrison, New Jersey, in August 1969. Amtrak is still nearly two years away, but the Northeast corridor did have a heavy traffic volume. *William Raia*

This photo by R. Yanosey was taken at Elizabeth, New Jersey, in October 1967. This Pennsy train has a consist of only five cars. This provides a good view of the four-track main line, which handled a wide mixture of train traffic. Through passenger trains to Washington as well as to Philadelphia, Pittsburgh and beyond, an extensive commuter train service plus numerous freight trains traveled the route daily. The Northeast corridor in 2008 is handling a record number of passengers. *William Raia Collection*

The PRR electrified route between New York and Philadelphia and beyond was a four-track Main line. This permitted a balanced scheduling system for the wide variety of trains through the corridor with the ability for on time performance. Not only did the Pennsylvania Railroad operate New York – Philadelphia – Washington, D.C. train services, but also many types of long distance trains such as the Broadway Limited. This particular train is the Silver Meteor, a Seaboard Florida Train, operating at speed at Elizabeth, New Jersey, in December 1968. *Jay Williams Collection*

Commuter trains were also part of the PRR service picture on the Northeast corridor. A New York City bound commuter train with eight cars is rolling through North Rahway, New Jersey, on the newly merged Penn Central in December 1969 on a cold and clear day. *Jay Williams Collection*

New York City – Philadelphia "Clocker" powered by the GG No. 4871 departs Penn Station in Newark with a generous shot of sand to get the train moving rapidly. *Photo by P. Buchent, Jay Williams Collection*

The Pennsy main line between New York and Washington, D. C., varied with four-track and triple-track main line segments. This photo illustrates part of a three-track section with the suburban station platforms on the outside tracks. *Jay Williams Collection*

Here is another example of the long distance train to Florida, the southbound Silver Meteor at Lincoln Tower in New Jersey in September 1966. *Michael L. Mc Bride*

The northbound Senator with Budd-built streamlined equipment, a complete consist of 15 cars, is shown here at Monmouth Junction, New Jersey, on the Penn Central — days before Amtrak — on April 24, 1971. *Michael L. Mc Bride*

Here is the westbound Pennsylvania Limited at Lincoln Tower in New Jersey in September 1966. The Pennsylvania Limited was a long distance train between Chicago and New York City. *Michael L. Mc Bride*

The Keystone was a newly designed low level type of passenger equipment, which operated in the Northeast corridor. It was built by the Budd Company, but no further orders were ever placed for the design. The train is shown here at Philadelphia in September 1966. *Michael L. Mc Bride*

Moving into the 1960s, the Pennsylvania Railroad purchased new passenger equipment for the various suburban services. The cars, built by the Budd Company, were attractive and very efficient. The portrait of the 201 was taken in 1963. *Harold K. Vollrath Collection*

The next step for the main line passenger service was the new Metroliners. The new equipment provided coach and parlor car seating as well as food and beverage service. This writer, while riding the new equipment, had the opportunity to time the speed. Two mileposts went by in 60 seconds. Yes, indeed it was 120 miles per hour. Car 800 is a cab car and its 1967 portrait illustrates the PRR's Keystone insignia. *Harold K. Vollrath Collection*

Car No. 852 is a Snack Bar coach and illustrates the new Penn Central insignia in this February, 1968 photo. *Harold K. Vollrath Collection*

Metroliner No. 888 is a Metro Club Car, the name for the parlor car services on the New Metroliners during the late 1960s. This portrait was taken at Trenton, New Jersey, in September 1968. *Harold K. Vollrath Collection*

Close-up view of the Penn Central 852 illustrating the new automatic couplers with all electrical and brake system connections. *The Budd Company Photo, Patrick C. Dorin Collection*

Table 10 of the Pennsylvania Railroad's January 26, 1967, schedule illustrates the eastbound through trains between Washington and New York. This is one route in the United States that now in 2008 has far more trains than 40 years ago.

20

WASHINGTON AND BALTIMORE TO PHILADELPHIA AND NEW YORK

Table **10** — *Eastern Standard Time* (Sleeping Cars (see below); Train Phone)

Miles	Station	The Edison 108 Daily	The Colonial to Boston 170 Daily	The Legislator 126 Daily	The Senator to Boston 172 Daily	The Midday Congressional 130 Daily	The Patriot to Boston 174 Daily	The Representative 132 Daily	The Afternoon Congressional 152 Except Saturdays
		AM	AM N.B.	AM N.L.B.	AM N.B.	AM N.B.	PM N.B.	PM N.B.	PM N.B.
.0	Lv **Washington, D. C.**	2.00	7.00	8.30	10.00	11.45	1.45	3.00	4.00
40.1	" **Baltimore, Md.** (Penna. Station)	2.40	7.45	9.10	10.40	12.26	2.26	3.41	4.40
70.3	" Aberdeen, Md	---	---	9.37	---	---	---	---	---
76.3	" Perryville, Md. (■Bainbridge)	---	---	---	---	---	---	---	---
90.6	" Elkton, Md	---	---	---	---	---	---	---	---
108.5	" Wilmington, Del	3.55	8.46	10.14	11.41	1.30	3.27	4.41	5.39
121.8	" Chester, Pa	---	---	---	---	---	---	---	---
----	Ar **Philadelphia, Pa.** (Penna. Sta. 30th St.)	4.32	9.15	10.43	12.09	1.58	3.55	5.09	6.06
135.2	Ar Philadelphia, Pa. (▲Suburban Sta.)	---	---	---	---	---	---	---	---
----	Lv **Philadelphia, Pa.** (Penna. Sta. 30th St.)	4.32	9.15	10.43	12.14	2.00	4.00	5.09	6.06
140.7	Ar **North Philadelphia, Pa**	4.52	9.25	1C.52	12.23	2.09	4.10	5.18	6.14
168.5	" Trenton, N. J	5.20	9.55	11 20	12.51	2.38	4.39	5.47	---
193.9	" New Brunswick, N. J	---	---	---	---	---	---	---	---
216.6	Ar **Newark, N. J**	d6.10	10.40	d12.05	1.35	3.22	5.24	6.30	7.20
216.6	Lv Newark, N. J	v6.11	v10.41	12.06	1.36	3.31	5.32	6.32	7.21
224.2	Ar Jersey City, N. J. (Exchange Place) (**u**)	v6.28	v10.58	12.28	1.58	3.48	5.49	6.48	7.38
225.4	" New York, N. Y. (Hudson Term.) (**u**)	v6.31	v11.01	12.31	2.01	3.51	5.52	6.51	7.41
226.6	Ar **New York, N. Y.** (Penna. Sta.)	6.50 AM	10.55 AM	12.20 PM	1.50 PM	3.35 PM	5.40 PM	6.45 PM	7.35 PM

Table **10** (Continued) — *Eastern Standard Time* (Sleeping Cars to Boston (see below))

Station	The Afternoon Congressional 162 Saturdays only	⊕ 400 Except Sat. & Sun.	The Embassy 154 Except Saturdays	The Mount Vernon 164 Saturdays & Sundays	The Mount Vernon 156 Except Sat. & Sun.	The Evening Keystone 166 Sundays only	The Evening Keystone 158 Except Sundays	The President 160 Daily	The Federal to Boston 176 Except Saturdays
	PM N.B.	PM	PM N.B.	PM N.B.	PM N.B.	PM N.B.	PM N.B.	PM	PM N.L.B.
Lv **Washington, D. C.**	4.30	4.30	5.00	6.00	6.00	7.30	7.30	9.15	10.20
" **Baltimore, Md.** (Penna. Station)	5.15	5.28	5.45	6.44	6.43	8.11	8.11	10.00	11.01
" Aberdeen, Md	---	6.01	---	---	---	---	---	---	---
" Perryville, Md. (■Bainbridge)	---	6.13	---	---	---	---	---	---	---
" Elkton, Md	---	---	---	---	---	---	---	---	---
" Wilmington, Del	6.14	7.05	6.48	7.45	7.47	9.12	9.12	11.03	12.07
" Chester, Pa	---	---	---	---	---	9.26	9.26	---	---
Ar **Philadelphia, Pa.** (Penna. Sta. 30th St.)	6.41	7.33	7.17	8.14	8.19	9.43	9.43	11.32	12.36
Ar Philadelphia, Pa. (▲Suburban Sta.)	---	---	---	---	---	---	---	---	---
Lv **Philadelphia, Pa.** (Penna. Sta. 30th St.)	6.41	---	7.17	8.14	8.19	9.43	9.43	11.40	1.03
Ar **North Philadelphia, Pa**	6.49	---	7.27	8.24	8.39	9.53	9.53	11.49	1.13
" Trenton, N. J	7.16	---	7.55	8.55	9.07	10.21	10.21	12.20	1.43
" New Brunswick, N. J	---	---	---	---	---	---	10.48	12.48	---
Ar **Newark, N. J**	8.00	---	8.40	9.39	9.53	11.05	11.15	1.09	2.29
Lv Newark, N. J	8.06	---	8.42	9.51	9.57	11.06	11.21	1.30	2.45
Ar Jersey City, N. J. (Exchange Place) (**u**)	8.22	---	8.58	10.07	10.13	11.22	11.43	1.46	3.01
" New York, N. Y. (Hudson Term.) (**u**)	8.25	---	9.01	10.10	10.16	11.25	11.46	1.49	3.04
Ar **New York, N. Y.** (Penna. Station)	8.15 PM	--- PM	8.55 PM	9.55 PM	10.15 PM	11.20 PM	11.30 PM	1.35 AM	2.50 AM

PARLOR, SLEEPING AND DINING CARS—(Table 10)
COACHES ON ALL TRAINS

No. 108—**Sleeping Cars**—Washington to New York—Roomettes and Double Bedrooms. Baltimore to New York—Roomettes and Double Bedrooms—Except Saturdays, Sundays and Feb. 22.
No. 126—Parlor Car, Parlor Room Bar Lounge Car, Dining Car and Snack Bar Coach—Hot-Cold Food and Beverages.
No. 130—Parlor Car, Dining (Bar Lounge) Car and Snack Bar Coach—Hot-Cold Food and Beverages.
No. 132—Parlor Car, Parlor Room Bar Lounge, Dining Car and Snack Bar Coach—Hot-Cold Food and Beverages.
No. 152—Parlor Car, Parlor Bar Lounge (Except Saturdays). Dining (Bar Lounge) Cars and Snack Bar Coach—Hot-Cold Food and Beverages.
No. 154—Parlor Car, Parlor Room Buffet Lounge Car and Snack Bar Coach—Hot-Cold Food and Beverages.
No. 156—Parlor Car, Parlor Room Bar Lounge Car, Dining Car and Snack Bar Coach—Hot-Cold Food and Beverages.
No. 158—Parlor Room Buffet Lounge Car and Refreshment Bar Service.
No. 160—Parlor Car—Washington to Philadelphia. (Except Feb. 21). Sleeping Car—Washington to Boston (Saturdays only) and Snack Bar Coach—Hot-Cold Food and Beverages. (Except Feb. 21).
No. 162—Parlor Car, Dining (Bar Lounge) Car and Snack Bar Coach—Hot-Cold Food and Beverages.
No. 164—Parlor Car, Parlor Room Bar Lounge Car, Dining Car and Snack Bar Coach—Hot-Cold Food and Beverages.
No. 166—Parlor Room Buffet Lounge Car and Refreshment Bar Service.
No. 170—Parlor Car, Parlor Bar Lounge Car, Dining Car and Snack Bar Coach—Hot-Cold Food and Beverages.
No. 172—Parlor Car, Parlor Room Bar Lounge Car and Dining Car.
No. 174—Parlor Car, Parlor Room Bar Lounge Car and Dining Car—♣.
No. 176—Sleeping Cars Washington to Boston, Philadelphia to Boston, Washington to New York—Roomettes and Double Bedroom) (Except Fridays, Saturdays, and Feb. 21). (In No. 108 from Baltimore, arrives New York 6.50 A.M.) Buffet Lounge

Drawing Rooms are available in Parlor Cars between Washing

For Reference Marks—

Go Pennsy—*Arrive refreshed* . . . Have an

22

WASHINGTON, BALTIMORE, PHILADELPHIA AND BOSTON

Table **12** — **Via Hell Gate Bridge Route** — **EASTWARD** — *Eastern Standard Time*

Miles	Station	The Colonial 170 Daily	The Senator 172 Daily	The Patriot 174 Daily	152-168 Except Sat.	162-168 Sat. only	The Federal 160-176 Sat. only	The Federal 176 Except Sat.
	Pennsylvania Railroad	AM N.B.	AM N.B.	PM N.B.	PM N.P.	PM N.P.	PM	PM N.W.
.0	Lv **Washington, D. C.**	7.00	10.00	1.45	4.00	4.30	9.15	10.20
40.1	" Baltimore, Md. (Pa. Sta.)	7.45	10.40	2.26	4.40	5.15	10.00	11.01
108.5	" Wilmington, Del.	8.46	11.41	3.27	5.39	6.14	11.03	12.07
----	" Phila. Pa. Penna. Sta. (30th St.)	9.15	12.14	4.00	6.06	6.41	11.40	1.03
140.7	" North Philadelphia, Pa.	9.25	12.23	4.10	6.14	6.49	11.49	1.13
216.6	" Newark, N. J.	10.40	1.35	5.24	7.20	8.00	1.09	2.29
226.6	Ar **New York, N. Y. (Penna. Sta.)**	10.55	1.50	5.40	7.35	8.15	1.35	2.50
	New Haven R. R.							
226.6	Lv **New York, N. Y. (Penna. Sta.)**	11.20	2.10	6.00	8.30	8.30	3.15	3.15
262.6	Ar Stamford, Conn.	12.06	2.56	6.46	9.24	9.24	---	---
285.1	" Bridgeport, Conn.	12.33	3.22	7.12	9.56	9.56	4.26	---
301.6	Ar New Haven, Conn.	12.51	3.40	7.30	10.15	10.15	4.44	4.44
301.6	Lv New Haven, Conn.	z 2.33	t 4.10	7.55	10.29	10.29	8.10	5.05
338.1	Ar Hartford, Conn.	z 3.21	t 5.05	8.49	11.22	11.22	9.04	6.09
363.6	Ar Springfield, Mass.	z 4.01	t 5.50	9.32	12.10	12.10	9.51	7.10
301.6	Lv New Haven, Conn.	12.59	3.48	7.38	v 10.49	v 11.56	5.07	5.07
334.6	Ar Old Saybrook, Conn.	---	4.22	---	v 11.24	v 12.31	---	---
352.6	" New London, Conn.	1.52	4.44	8.31	v 11.45	v 12.52	6.01	6.01
370.6	" Westerly, R. I.	---	5.08	8.53	---	---	6.31	6.31
387.6	" Kingston, R. I.	---	5.26	---	---	---	6.50	6.50
414.6	" Providence, R. I.	2.53	5.55	9.37	v 12.50	v 2.00	7.17	7.17
446.6	" Route 128, Mass. ♦	3.26	6.26	10.10	v 1.32	v 2.45	8.03	8.03
----	Ar **Boston, Mass.** **Back Bay**	3.40	6.40	10.25	v 1.45	v 2.58	8.20	8.20
458.6	**South Sta.**	3.45 PM	6.45 PM	10.30 PM	v 1.50 AM	v 3.03 AM	8.25 AM	8.25 AM

Reference Marks

Note 1.—Runs except Saturdays and Sundays.
Note 2.—Runs except Sundays and Feb 22.
E.S.T. Eastern Standard Time.
N.B No checked baggage handled on this train.
N.B.N. No checked baggage Boston to New York; no local checked baggage between New York and Washington.
N.P. No checked baggage south of New York.
N.W. No local checked baggage between New York and Washington.
§ Sundays only.
† Except Sundays.
♦ No checked baggage handled at this station.
◆ Sandwiches-Snacks-Beverages available at your coach seat only in area between Washington and New York.
♣ Sandwiches-Snacks-Beverages available at your coach seat only in area between Philadelphia and New York.
♥ Sandwiches-Snacks-Beverages available at your coach seat only in area between Philadelphia and Washington.
c Stops only to receive passengers.
e On Sundays leave Springfield 10.30 a.m., Hartford 11.01 a.m. arrive New Haven 11.49 a.m.
g On Sundays leave Springfield 9.00 a.m., Hartford 9.31 a.m. arrive New Haven 10.20 a.m.
n On Sundays and Feb. 22, leave Springfield 9.12 p.m. Hartford 9.54 p.m., arrive New Haven 10.48 p.m.
q Sundays and Feb. 22.
r On Feb. 22, leave Springfield 9.12 p.m., Hartford 9.54 p.m., arrives New Haven 10.48 p.m.
t On Sundays leave New Haven 4.05 p.m., arrive Hartford 4.56 p.m. and Springfield 5.28 p.m.
v By connecting train from New Haven.
y By connecting train, change trains at New Haven.
z On Sundays leave New Haven 2.26 p.m., arrive Hartford 3.16 p.m. and Springfield 3.50 p.m.

WESTWARD — *Eastern Standard Time*

Station	169-115 Daily	The Hell Gate 181 See Note 2	The Colonial 171 Daily	The Senator 173 Daily	The Patriot 175 Daily	The Pilgrim 199 Sun. only	The Pilgrim 197 Sat. only	The Pilgrim 179 See Note 1	The Federal 177 Except Sat.	The New Yorker 185-131 Sun. only	The New Yorker 187-131 See Note 1	The New Yorker 187-111 Sat. only
New Haven R. R.	AM N.P.	AM	AM N.B.N.	AM N.B.	PM N.B.	PM	PM	PM N.B.	PM N.W.	PM N.B.	PM N.P.	PM N.P.
Lv **Boston, Mass.** **South Sta.**	y 2.00	6.45	8.00	10.00	1.00	9.00	9.00	9.00	10.10	11.45	11.45	11.45
Back Bay	y 2.05	6.50	8.05	10.05	1.05	9.05	9.05	9.10	10.15	11.50	11.50	11.50
" Route 128, Mass. ♦	y 2.26	7.02	8.18	10.21	1.19	9.22	9.22	9.30	10.30	12.05	12.07	12.07
" Providence, R. I.	y 3.20	8.00	8.54	10.56	1.55	10.12	10.25	10.45	11.10	1.06	1.26	1.26
" Kingston, R. I.	---	8.27	---	11.22	---	10.40	10.53	11.12	---	---	---	---
" Westerly, R. I.	---	8.45	---	---	---	10.58	11.13	11.30	---	---	---	---
" New London, Conn.	y 4.35	9.14	9.54	11.59	2.55	11.25	11.47	11.58	c12.10	2.13	2.37	2.37
Lv Old Saybrook, Conn.	---	9.36	---	12.20	3.16	11.47	12.09	12.20	---	---	---	---
Ar New Haven, Conn.	y 5.34	10.10	10.46	12.54	3.50	12.23	12.45	12.55	1.04	3.08	3.33	3.33
Lv Springfield, Mass.	5.00	7.21	g 9.30	e 10.05	2.35	9.12	9.38	r 9.10	n 9.10	12.00	12.40	12.40
" Hartford, Conn.	5.35	8.00	g10.01	e 10.50	3.06	9.54	10.18	r10.03	n10.03	12.37	1.34	1.34
Ar New Haven, Conn.	6.22	8.51	g10.48	e 11.49	3.53	10.48	11.13	r11.11	n11.11	1.32	2.33	2:33
Lv New Haven, Conn.	6.35	10.25	10.54	1.03	3.58	12.36	1.03	1.20	1.27	3.23	4.08	4.08
" Bridgeport, Conn.	6.56	10.46	11.14	1.23	4.19	12.54	1.20	1.37	---	3.46	4.26	4.26
" Stamford, Conn.	q 7.20	11.13	11.38	1.50	q 4.42	1.32	1.57	2.18	---	4.15	4.56	4.56
Ar **New York (Penna. Sta.)**	8.10	12.00	12.25	2.40	5.25	2.40	3.00	3.35	2.55	5.10	6.00	6.00
Pennsylvania R. R.												
Lv **New York, N. Y. (Penna. Sta.)**	9.30	---	12.45	3.00	5.45	---	---	---	3.23	6.30	6.30	8.00
Ar Newark, N. J.	9.46	---	1.01	3.16	6.01	---	---	---	3.38	6.45	6.45	8.16
" North Philadelphia, Pa.	10.56	---	2.13	4.29	7.15	---	---	---	4.57	8.00	8.00	9.26
" Phila., Pa., Penna. Sta. (30th St.)	11.05	---	2.22	4.39	7.24	---	---	---	5.09	8.10	8.10	9.35
" Wilmington, Del.	11.37	---	2.53	5.08	7.52	---	---	---	5.46	8.38	8.38	10.08
" Baltimore, Md. (Penna. Sta.)	12.38	---	3.58	6.09	8.53	---	---	---	6.53	9.39	9.39	11.09
Ar **Washington, D. C.**	1.20 PM	--- Noon	4.40 PM	6.50 PM	9.35 PM	--- AM	--- AM	--- AM	7.45 AM	10.20 AM	10.20 AM	11.50 AM

Go places together...at worthwhile savings! Ask about Pennsy Family Fares.

The Pennsy's 1967 timetable listed the through trains between Washington, D. C., and Boston. There were more westbound trains than eastbound that year.

The equipment listings for the Washington – Boston services in 1967. PRR Time Table, Jan. 29, 1967, p. 23.

The New York – Philadelphia segment had far more trains than the remainder of the PRR route to Washington. Table 13 from the Jan. 29, 1967, issue also lists the equipment and accommodations for the service.

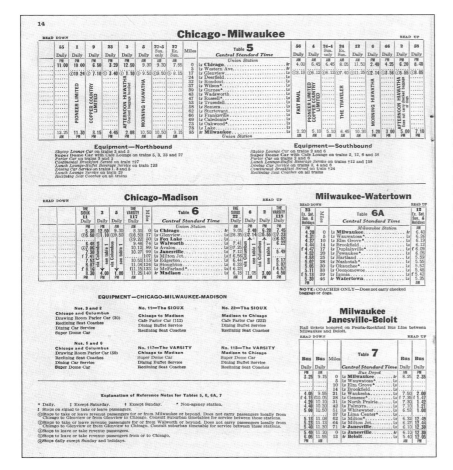

The Milwaukee Road and the Chicago and North Western plus the Chicago, North Shore and Milwaukee served the Chicago – Milwaukee corridor. Page 24 of the April 26, 1964, Milwaukee Road Time Table illustrates the service level between Chicago and Milwaukee. At that time there were 15 daily trains on the schedule. It did not list the Fast Mail to Minneapolis, which did not carry coach passengers on the westbound run. As of 2008, Amtrak operates 8 trains per day between Chicago and Milwaukee. Other information on Page 14 illustrates the Chicago – Madison service plus the commuter train between Milwaukee and Watertown, Wisconsin.

We will begin the pictorial review of local passenger services by taking a look at the consist of a train from 1868. This 4-4-0 steam engine, the first to be converted from wood to coal, was leading two coaches at Crestwood, New York, on the New York and Harlem Railroad. During that period of history, the two-car consist was typical of many trains which stopped at virtually every station along the routes. The history of the local passenger service began with the start of the railroad industry around 1830. *Harold K. Vollrath Collection*

CHAPTER 2

LOCAL TRAIN OPERATIONS

The local passenger train schedule was a service that stopped at nearly every station along the route. Towns or stations that did not have a scheduled stop in the timetable did have a "flag stop" designation. Passengers would arrive at the depot, often simply a shelter, and could alert the engineer of the oncoming train by either waving their arm or even a flag. At night, a flashlight was needed and hopefully the engineer would see the light. Passengers onboard a train, and who needed to get off at a flag stop, would tell the conductor what their destination station was. Often, the conductor could tell by simply looking at the passenger's ticket if they had one. On many local runs, passengers could pay for the ticket on the train. However, for most cities and towns, the stations did have an agent for selling train tickets.

Local trains had many different types of equipment consists as well as the type of service. For ex-

ample, many local trains operated over the main line providing connecting service for the long distance trains to the many locations. In this case, the local would operate behind a limited train, and pick up passengers at various stations to drop off at destinations a few miles ahead. The same could be true for passengers to catch a local train at a non-stop location for a limited train, and then get off at a location up the line to catch the longer distance run. These are only two examples of main line operations.

There were many long distance trains that operated as a limited on parts of the route, and then as a local the remainder of the route. Two examples included the Chicago and North Western's Ashland Limited between Chicago and Green Bay, which served all of the local stops between Green Bay and Ashland. Believe it or not, the Flambeau 400 did the same type of operation between Green Bay and Ashland, although it did not make as many stops as the Ashland Limited. The Ashland Limited provided the overnight service while the Flambeau 400 was the day train.

Local trains also provided branch line service. The main line train would stop at the branch line station junction, and passenger could detrain and transfer to the local for their destination. Or passengers could catch the local on the branch and ride to the junction to transfer to the main line train.

Another type of local passenger service was the mixed train. This type of train provided both freight and passenger service, usually over a branch line.

Local train equipment consists varied depending upon the type of service. Quite frequently, the local was equipped with one baggage car, or one Railway Post Office-baggage car, and one or two coaches. There were local trains as short as one car. One example was the Soo Line's Duluth – Thief River Falls local train, which consisted of one Railway Post Office-baggage-coach.

Many local trains were equipped with gas-electric cars, which often consisted of simply one car equipped with coach seating and mail and baggage areas. There were many gas-electric runs throughout North America which were equipped with one gas-electric car with only mail and baggage compartments, and one or two trailer coaches.

Mixed trains generally operated with one combination baggage-coach on the rear of the train. However, there were some mixed trains that were equipped with a baggage car and one coach on the rear of the train. One example of such a train was the mixed train service on the Canadian National between Thunder Bay and Sioux Lookout, Ontario.

Motive power for the local trains originally consisted of the smaller types of steam power. Steam engines, such as 2-6-0s or 4-6-2s, were more than powerful enough to handle the one- to five- or six-car consists that were common for local services. The steam power was eventually replaced by diesel power. Single unit F-3s or F-7s built by Electro-Motive Division were quite common, but even more so were the road-switcher types such as GP-7s or 9s from EMD, or the Alco RS-3s.

The local train services were literally among the first group of passenger train services to disappear due to the influx of the automobile. They were North

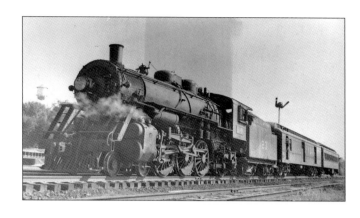

The two-car local passenger trains, either steam or diesel powered, can be quite convenient for model railroaders – known as Pike Size trains. This illustration views a Louisville and Nashville local with one RPO-baggage (with a 15-foot Rail Post Office section) and one coach. The train is pausing at Jena, Tennessee. Note the semaphore signal in the background. This happens to be a "Train Order." One blade is in the clear position, while the other (which is facing toward the head of the train) in the caution position indicates a train order is to be picked up by a train in the opposite direction at Jena. This could mean a change of a siding location for a meet with an opposing train. *Harold K. Vollrath Collection*

America's shortest passenger trains, and, of course, carried the fewest number of passengers. The best bets for survival were the trains that connected with the longer distance operations.

An interesting aspect of the local trains was the sense of community that could be found onboard. Local train patronage had many repeat passengers, and people really knew one another. When this writer was employed by the Great Northern during my college years – late '50s and early '60s – it was really a pleasant ride on one of the GN locals between Grand Forks and Minot, North Dakota.

As of this writing in 2008, the only local train operations that can be found in North America are part of the commuter train services in the metropolitan areas.

Following are photos and timetables illustrating the Local Train Operations from the 1940s into the early 1960s.

Moving forward to the twentieth century, many of the local trains throughout North America consisted of just two cars, most often a Rail Post Office-baggage car and one or two coaches. This is a Baltimore and Ohio Railroad local pausing at Rochester, New York, in July 1950. The RPO-baggage car has a 15-foot Rail Post Office section, while the remainder of the car is devoted to Railway Express and passengers' baggage. The single coach was often sufficient for the ridership as it continued to decline from the 1930s on. *Harold K. Vollrath Collection*

Steam power for the local passenger trains, even into the 1940s, was often provided by the 4-4-2 Atlantics and the 4-6-2 Pacifics, such as the Bangor and Aroostook No. 254 shown here leading a train at Sherman, Maine, in July 1940. Note the open-end wooden baggage car behind the locomotive. The wood head-end cars were the last of such cars to operate in the passenger trains, with some exceptions, as the steel and far safer coach equipment was placed in operation. *Harold K. Vollrath Collection*

During the 1940s, the Chicago and North Western operated a local train between Chicago and Freeport, Illinois, over the main line and a branch line from West Chicago to Freeport. During the early 1940s, No. 703 was a morning departure at 8:20 a.m. from Chicago with a 5-hour, 5-minute running time to Freeport, a distance of 120.9 miles. Eastbound No. 706 departed Freeport at 3:35 p.m. for a four-hour run to Chicago. This view in 1947 shows the four-car consist pausing at Rockford, Illinois. *Harold K. Vollrath Collection*

Southern Pacific local No. 381 is shown here at Fort Thomas, Arizona, date unknown. During the 1940s, the SP operated 381 from Globe to Bowie, 124 miles on a 4-hour, 10-minute schedule in the morning. Eastbound 382 departed Bowie at 2:55 p.m. for a 4-hour, 10-minute run to Globe. (Photo by W. E. Miller, W. C. Whittaker Collection)

This Boston and Maine local's portrait was taken at Reading, Massachusetts, in April 1941. The steam power doing the honors is a 4-4-2 Atlantic and is heading up a consist of open-end wooden coaches. *Harold K. Vollrath Collection*

Bessemer and Lake Erie local trains 1 and 2 operated between Greenville and North Bessemer, Pennsylvania. Train No. 2 is heading for Greenville with a two-car consist including an RPO-Baggage with a 30-foot section for the Rail Post Office. The train is at Culmerville, Pennsylvania, in September 1948. *Harold K. Vollrath Collection*

The B&LE operated two sets of local trains, 1 and 2 (shown previously) and 11 and 12. No. 11 and 12 operated between Erie and Greenville. Depending upon traffic levels, the trains were equipped with one or two coaches, such as the train illustrated here powered by steam, the 903. *Richard Cook, Bob Lorenz Collection*

Local passenger trains were common in both rural and urban areas. In this case, a Duluth, South Shore & Atlantic Railway 4-6-2 is leading a local train west of Marquette, Michigan, with a three-car consist: Two Railway Post Office-Baggage cars and one coach. This was part of a train schedule that operated between St. Ignace and Calumet, Michigan. Consists of head-end equipment on local trains varied depending upon the amount of mail and Railway Express traffic. The South Shore also operated an overnight local between Marquette and Duluth, Minnesota, with a two-car consist including an RPO-Baggage and a combination sleeper-coach. This would often vary with an additional baggage car or a full coach. *Harold K. Vollrath Collection*

This local train on the Frisco Railroad is powered by a 4-4-0 steam locomotive with a two-car consist at Kansas City, Missouri, in July, 1947. The identity of this train is not certain, but it could be No. 112, which operated from Fort Scott to Kansas City on an early morning run making all stops. *Harold K. Vollrath Collection*

Train No. 9 on the former Denver and Salt Lake — later part of the Denver, Rio Grande and Western Railroad — operated as an overnight local between Denver and Craig in the early 1950s. The portrait of this two-car consist of No. 9 was taken at Plainview, Colorado, in July 1947. *Harold K. Vollrath Collection*

This Canadian Pacific Railway local train, No. 137, operated between Brandon, Manitoba, and Estevan, Saskatchewan. The train made all stops on its run over the 164.5-mile route. No. 137 operated west to Estevan in the late afternoon, and 138 departed Estevan early in the morning. The running time was 7 hours westbound and 6 hours eastbound with 19 stops in each direction during the 1950s. Note the consist of five head-end cars and one coach. (Jim Scribbins, Brandon, May 28, 1947)

Still another type of local passenger service was the Mixed Train, meaning a train providing both freight and passenger service. Mixed trains most often operated over branch lines, but there were main line operations too. Mixed trains generally had one or two passenger cars or a single car, such as this combination RPO-coach, Texas and New Orleans No. 407. The car operated on the rear of mixed trains No. 216, 217, 218 and 219, providing twice-daily service on the Harwood – Gonzales, Texas, branch line. The 12-mile route had 30-minute schedules for all four trains. *Harold K. Vollrath Collection*

Many local trains across North America operated with gas-electric power. One of the neatest trains operated on the Santa Fe with bright streamlined colors of silver and red with yellow striping. This articulated gas-electric handled one streamlined coach and is shown here at Carlsbad, New Mexico, in September 1958. *Herman Page*

Grand Truck Western gas-electric No. 15805 was a combination coach-RPO-Baggage car. The car operated on the local train between Detroit and Port Huron. The consist included one baggage car attached to the rear of the gas-electric. This photo was taken at Detroit in 1946. The two-car consist is ahead of two other cars between runs at the end of the station track but are not part of the Port Huron train, which operated to Detroit in the morning and to Port Huron in the afternoon. *Harold K. Vollrath Collection*

Other examples of gas-electric powered trains were the Chesapeake and Ohio's trains 50 and 51 between Huntington and Logan. Train 50 departed Huntington around 7:15 a.m. and took 3 hours, 10 minutes to make the run to Logan, a distance of 75 miles. Train 51 departed Logan about 3:25 p.m. and used only 2 hours, 55 minutes on the return trip. The combination Baggage-RPO-coach pulled an RPO-Baggage car as part of the consist on this route. *Bob Lorenz*

The C&O operated an RDC-1 coach, which pulled a combination Baggage-coach car on a local service between Newport News and Richmond, trains 47 and 48 during the 1960s. This was one example of the last types of locals operated on various routes prior to Amtrak. As one can understand, the local passenger trains were the first to be discontinued during the long period of decline in train services. *Bob Lorenz*

The New York Central operated an RDC-3 on its train service between Detroit and northern Michigan. The train is shown here at Cheboygan, Michigan, in February 1962. *Herman Page*

During the middle 1950s, the Canadian Pacific invested in Rail Diesel Cars for local train assignments in Canada. An RDC-2 (Combination coach-Baggage) and an RDC-4 (RPO-Baggage) operated on the route between Vanceboro and Edmundston, New Brunswick. The local train is shown here at Woodstock, New Brunswick. *Harold K. Vollrath Collection*

The Budd Company Rail Diesel Cars, such as the RDC-1 a full coach, were operated in both local and to a certain extent longer distance train services. One of the longest operations was on the Western Pacific between Oakland and Salt Lake City. The Canadian Pacific's subsidiary, the Esquemalt & Namaimo Railway on Victoria Island, operated Budd cars in local service between Victoria and Courtney. In this view, train No. 2 is ready to depart Courtney for Victoria. *Jim Scribbins*

Another type of RDC car assigned to local operations was the RDC-3, a Combination coach-Baggage-Rail Post Office car, such as the Canadian National's D-354 shown here at Kelowna, British Columbia. The RDC-3 was assigned to trains 193 and 194 during the early 1960s. The local operated between Kelowna and Kamloops, a distance of 118.9 miles. It was a morning run to Kelowna and the return to Kamloops in the afternoon. Trains 193 and 194 operated as connections to the Continental on the main line. *Harold K. Vollrath Collection*

Some of the most common local train services, of which many routes still exist, were the commuter routes. One example in Canada was the Canadian National commuter trains between Toronto and Hamilton. Rush hour local service was provided by three trains in each direction. Steam power, later replaced by diesel locomotives known as geeps from General Motors (Canada), along with steam generator cars provided the power for the trains. Also, 12 section, 1 Drawing Room sleeping cars were often operated as coaches on these trains. This route has been handled by GO Transit since 1967 with more commuter train schedules then ever in the history of the route. *Patrick C. Dorin, 1974*

Commuter train services were and are quite extensive. In fact, many of the routes now have more trains running in the 21st Century than they had in the 1940s and beyond to the 1990s. Just one example is the Southern Pacific route between San Francisco and San Jose, which now (2008) has 48 trains in each direction on weekdays, compared to 23 in each direction during the 1960s. This Illinois Central train illustrates the type of trains operated from the 1920s to the 1970s, and is in local service on the South Chicago Branch. *Bob Lorenz*

The Chicago and North Western and the Burlington pioneered the concept of bi-level gallery commuter coaches during the 1950s, '60s and beyond. This C&NW mid-day train is operating over the Northwest route from Chicago, and with its three-car consist is making all stops. A perfect example of a local passenger train in suburban service. *Thomas A. Dorin*

The C&NW pioneered the Push-Pull concept for commuter train service and this view illustrates the Cab coach at the end of the three-car consist. *Michael A. Dorin*

The bi-level passenger equipment was first designed and placed into operation on the Burlington Route's commuter train services in Chicago in the late 1940s and '50s. Later, other railroads adopted the concept, not only for commuter rail, but also for long distance service. The C&NW operated this type of equipment on the Flambeau and the Peninsula 400s between Chicago, and northern Wisconsin and Upper Michigan. The C&NW No. 33 is shown here in the consist of a "Local" commuter run at a station stop near Chicago. *Thomas A. Dorin*

The C&NW was one of the pioneers in replacing the steam powered systems (with steam generators in the diesel power), with what is known as Head-end Power, or HEP. Electric cables provide the electric power to the passenger consist for lighting, air-conditioning and heating. *Thomas A. Dorin*

As time went on through the 1950s and '60s, any local trains that survived were often reduced to a single-coach consist without any head-end cars or other equipment. Just one example was the Milwaukee Road's connection with the Hiawathas at New Lisbon, Wisconsin. and the route north to Wausau. The Milwaukee Road powered the single-car train with one FP-7. This Milwaukee Road coach No. 639 is shown here after operating on a passenger extra to Duluth, Minnesota. *Patrick C. Dorin*

The Soo Line Railroad offered a limited amount of passenger service on their route between Rhinelander and Gladstone and perhaps further east to Sault Ste. Marie. This was still in existence in the 1970s, and passengers were carried in a caboose. *Patrick C. Dorin*

When passengers wished to board a local passenger train at night, at a station without an agent or train order operator; the passenger needed to flag down the train with a flashlight. Such is the case here where a passenger is flagging down a Chicago, South Shore and South Bend Railroad train at Dune Park. *Frank Schnick*

To complete the chapter on the different types of local passenger train services, let's take a look at one of the local trains the Chicago and North Western once operated between Chicago and Milwaukee. The fast trains were making the run in 85 to 90 minutes, whereas the locals with steam power in the early 1950s did the run in about 2 hours, 30 minutes on average. This portrait at Milwaukee in June 1951 could be useful for model railroaders for a pike sized train with the Pacific type 4-6-2 for power and one baggage car and three coaches. All of the cars were in the 60-foot range. *William Raia*

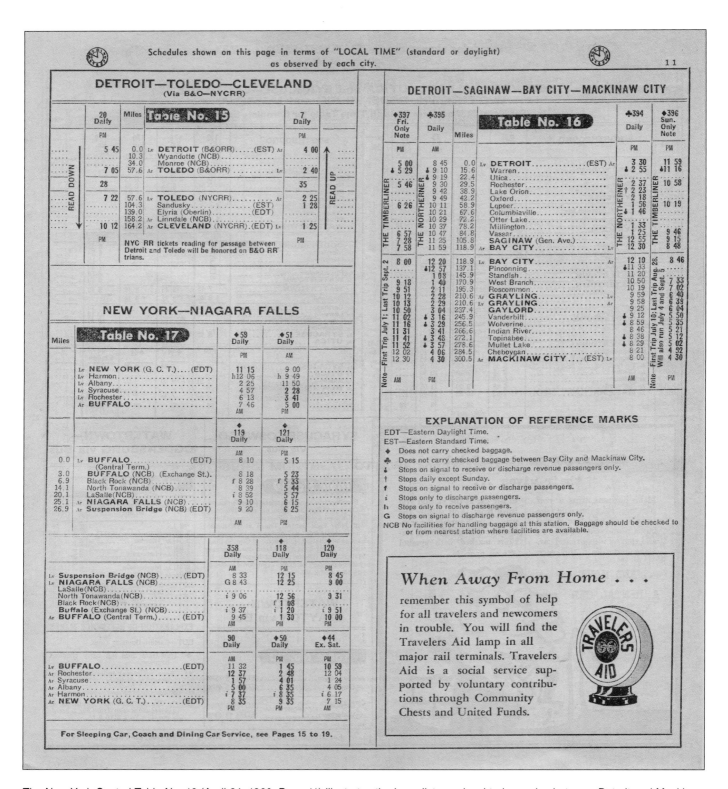

DETROIT—TOLEDO—CLEVELAND
(Via B&O—NYCRR)
Table No. 15

20 Daily	Miles		7 Daily
PM			PM
5 45	0.0	Lv DETROIT (B&ORR).....(EST) Ar	4 00
	10.3	Wyandotte (NCB)	
	34.0	Monroe (NCB)	
7 05	57.6	Ar TOLEDO (B&ORR) Lv	2 40
28			35
7 22	57.6	Lv TOLEDO (NYCRR) Ar	2 25
	104.3	Sandusky (EST)	1 28
	139.0	Elyria (Oberlin) (EDT)	
	158.2	Ar Linndale (NCB)	
10 12	164.2	Ar CLEVELAND (NYCRR) (EDT) Lv	1 25
PM			PM

NYC RR tickets reading for passage between Detroit and Toledo will be honored on B&O RR trians.

NEW YORK—NIAGARA FALLS
Table No. 17

Miles		◆59 Daily	◆51 Daily
		PM	AM
	Lv NEW YORK (G. C. T.)....(EDT)	11 15	9 00
	Lv Harmon	h12 06	h 9 49
	Lv Albany	2 25	11 50
	Lv Syracuse	4 57	2 28
	Lv Rochester	6 13	3 41
	Ar BUFFALO	7 46	5 00
		AM	PM

Miles		119 Daily	121 Daily
		AM	PM
0.0	Lv BUFFALO (Central Term.) (EDT)	8 10	5 15
3.0	BUFFALO (NCB) (Exchange St.)	8 18	5 23
6.9	Black Rock (NCB)	f 8 28	f 5 33
14.1	North Tonawanda (NCB)	8 39	5 44
20.1	LaSalle(NCB)	i 8 52	5 57
25.1	Ar NIAGARA FALLS (NCB)	9 10	6 15
26.9	Ar Suspension Bridge (NCB) (EDT)	9 20	6 25
		AM	PM

		358 Daily	118 Daily	120 Daily
		AM	PM	PM
	Lv Suspension Bridge (NCB) (EDT)	8 33	12 15	8 45
	Lv NIAGARA FALLS (NCB)	G 8 43	12 25	9 00
	LaSalle(NCB)			
	North Tonawanda (NCB)	i 9 06	12 56	9 31
	Black Rock(NCB)		f 1 08	
	Buffalo (Exchange St.) (NCB)	i 9 37		i 9 51
	Ar BUFFALO (Central Term.) (EDT)	9 45	1 30	10 00
		AM	PM	PM

		90 Daily	◆50 Daily	◆44 Ex. Sat.
		AM	PM	PM
	Lv BUFFALO (EDT)	11 32	1 45	10 59
	Ar Rochester	12 37	2 48	12 04
	Ar Syracuse	1 57	4 01	1 24
	Ar Albany	5 00	6 35	4 05
	Ar Harmon	i 7 37	i 8 35	i 6 17
	Ar NEW YORK (G. C. T.) (EDT)	8 35	9 35	7 15
		PM	PM	AM

For Sleeping Car, Coach and Dining Car Service, see Pages 15 to 19.

DETROIT—SAGINAW—BAY CITY—MACKINAW CITY
Table No. 16

Note—First Trip July 1; Last Trip Sept. 2
Note—First Trip July 10; Last Trip Aug. 28. Will also run July 4 and Sept. 5

◆337 Fri. Only Note	♣395 Daily	Miles		◆394 Daily	◆396 Sun. Only Note
PM	AM			PM	PM
5 00	8 45	0.0	Lv DETROIT (EST) Ar	3 30	11 59
♪5 29	♪9 10	15.6	Warren	2 55	♪11 16
	9 19	22.4	Utica		
5 46	9 30	29.5	Rochester	2 37	10 58
	9 42	38.9	Lake Orion	2 23	
	9 49	42.2	Oxford	2 18	
6 26	10 11	58.9	Lapeer	1 56	10 19
	10 21	67.6	Columbiaville	♪1 46	
	10 29	72.2	Otter Lake		
	10 37	78.2	Millington	1 33	
6 57	10 47	84.8	Vassar	12 55	9 46
7 28	11 25	105.8	SAGINAW (Gen. Ave.)	12 30	9 15
7 58	11 59	118.9	Ar BAY CITY Lv		8 48
8 00	12 20	118.9	Lv BAY CITY Ar	12 10	8 46
	♪12 57	137.1	Pinconning	♪11 33	
	1 08	145.9	Standish	11 20	
9 18	1 40	170.9	West Branch	10 50	7 33
	2 11	195.3	Roscommon	10 19	7 02
10 12	2 28	210.6	Ar GRAYLING Lv	9 59	6 40
10 13	2 29	210.6	Lv GRAYLING Ar	9 58	6 39
10 50	3 04	237.4	GAYLORD	9 25	6 04
11 02	3 16	245.9	Vanderbilt	♪9 12	♪5 55
11 16	3 29	256.5	Wolverine	8 59	5 35
	3 41	266.6	Indian River	8 46	5 21
11 41	3 48	272.1	Topinabee	♪8 38	♪5 12
11 52	3 57	278.6	Mullet Lake	♪8 29	♪5 02
12 02	4 06	284.5	Cheboygan	8 21	4 52
12 30	4 30	300.5	Ar MACKINAW CITY (EST) Lv	8 00	4 30
AM	PM			AM	PM

EXPLANATION OF REFERENCE MARKS

EDT—Eastern Daylight Time.
EST—Eastern Standard Time.
◆ Does not carry checked baggage.
♣ Does not carry checked baggage between Bay City and Mackinaw City.
♪ Stops on signal to receive or discharge revenue passengers only.
† Stops daily except Sunday.
f Stops on signal to receive or discharge passengers.
i Stops only to discharge passengers.
h Stops only to receive passengers.
G Stops on signal to discharge revenue passengers only.
NCB No facilities for handling baggage at this station. Baggage should be checked to or from nearest station where facilities are available.

The New York Central Table No. 16 (April 24, 1960, Page 11) illustrates the long distance local train service between Detroit and Mackinaw City. The day schedule was known as the Northerner. Table No. 16 also shows a special weekend train, known as the Timberliner, which operated an afternoon schedule northbound on Fridays, and southbound on Sundays during the summer.

New York Central

TIME TABLE

SUBURBAN TRAIN SERVICE

CHICAGO

La Salle St. Station

ENGLEWOOD
GIBSON
GARY
CHESTERTON
LA PORTE
and
INTERMEDIATE STATIONS

•

Effective December 5, 1948

The New York Central also published timetables illustrating the local and/ or commuter services, such as this schedule of suburban trains between Chicago and La Porte, Indiana. The suburban train numbers were listed as the 600 series, while the through trains had the long distance train numbers. It is interesting to note that this December 5, 1948, timetable advertised some of the long distance trains and included both steam and diesel power as part of the insignia.

SUBURBAN TRAINS CHICAGO TO GIBSON, CHESTERTON AND LA PORTE

CENTRAL STANDARD TIME Eastbound	664 Daily	52 Daily	650 Daily Except Sunday	654 Daily	656 Daily	608 Daily Except Sunday	232 Daily	680 Sat. Only	672 Daily Except Sat. & Sunday	98 Daily	644 Daily Except Sat. & Sunday	612 Daily Except Sat. & Sunday	660 Daily Except Sunday	616 Sat. & Sunday only	10 Daily	662 Daily	62 Daily	290 Daily
	AM	AM	AM	AM	AM	AM	AM	PM	PM	PM	PM	PM	PM	PM	PM	PM	PM	PM
0 Lv Chicago (La Salle St. Sta.)		12.50	5.00	6.30		8.40	11.35	1.40	1.45	3.30	4.40	5.20	5.30	5.40		10.30	10.45	11.30
6.6 Lv Englewood (63rd St.)			5.13	6.43		8.54	11.49	1.53	1.58	3.44	4.55	5.33	5.43	5.54		10.43	10.59	11.44
7.7 Lv Park Manor (69th St.)			5.16	6.46				1.56	2.01		4.59		5.46			10.46		
8.1 Lv 71st Street			5.18	6.48				1.58	2.03				5.49			10.49		
11.8 Lv South Chicago (92nd St.)			5.25	6.55			B 11.57	2.04	2.09		5.06		5.56			10.55		
13.1 Lv East Side (100th St.)			5.28	6.59				2.07	2.12		5.09		6.00	6.00		10.58		
15.5 Lv Robertsdale (116th St.)			5.33	7.03				2.10	2.15		5.13		6.05	6.05		11.03		
16.7 Lv Whiting (119th St.)	12.25		5.38	7.07	8.30		12.04	2.13	2.18		5.17		6.09	6.09		11.07	11.11	
18.6 Lv Mahoning (125th St.)	12.29		5.43	7.10	8.34			2.17	2.22		5.22			f 6.12		11.11		
19.3 Lv Indiana Harbor (132nd St.)	12.32		5.45	7.15	8.36		9.10	12.10	2.20	2.25	5.25	5.48		6.15		11.14	11.16	
23.4 Ar Gibson																	11.27	
21.1 Lv Buffington (137th St.)	12.35		5.49	7.20	8.39			2.23	2.28		5.29	5.51		6.18		11.18		
22.9 Lv Pine			f 5.52	7.24				2.27	2.32					f 6.22				
23.9 Lv Curtis			5.55	7.26														
25.3 Lv Kirk Yard	12.42		5.58	7.30	8.47			2.32	2.37		5.37					11.25		
26.1 Lv Gary	12.44	1.23	6.02	7.35	8.50		9.20	12.20	2.35	2.40	5.40	6.03		6.30	6.13	11.30		
29.7 Lv Millers	12.49				8.56				2.41		5.46	6.09		6.36				
33.8 Lv Ogden Dunes	f 12.54				f 9.01				2.46		5.52	6.13		6.41				
35.4 Lv Dune Park					f 9.05				2.49			f 6.16		f 6.44				
40.2 Lv Porter	1.03				9.11				2.55		6.01	6.23		6.51				
41.0 Ar Chesterton	1.05				9.15		9.35	12.36	3.00		6.05	6.25		6.55				
58.8 Ar La Porte		2.00					10.00	1.05		C 4.35					6.50			12.30
	AM	AM	AM	AM	AM	AM	AM	PM	PM	PM	PM	PM	PM	PM	PM	PM	PM	AM

SUBURBAN TRAINS LA PORTE, CHESTERTON AND GIBSON TO CHICAGO

CENTRAL STANDARD TIME Westbound	663 Daily Except Sun. & Monday	665 Sunday & Mon. Only	9 Daily	5 Daily	63 Daily	653 Daily	651 Daily Except Sunday	641 Daily Ex. Sun.	257 Daily	657 Daily	35 Daily	681 Sat. Only	673 Daily Except Sat. & Sunday	661 Daily Except Sat. & Sunday	687 Sat. & Sunday Only
	AM	AM	AM	AM	AM	AM	AM	AM	PM	PM	PM	PM	PM	PM	PM
Lv La Porte			4.10	5.32					1.05		3.25				
Lv Chesterton	12.05					6.30				2.30		4.05		10.30	10.30
Lv Porter	12.07					6.33				2.33		4.07		10.32	10.32
Lv Dune Park										2.39		f 4.13		f 10.37	f 10.37
Lv Ogden Dunes	f 12.12					f 6.42				2.42		f 4.16		f 10.40	f 10.40
Lv Millers						6.47				2.47		f 4.21		10.45	10.45
Lv Gary	12.25	12.25	5.05	6.22		6.53	6.42	7.25		2.55		4.35	4.35	10.50	10.50
Lv Kirk Yard	12.27	12.27				6.55				2.58		4.38	4.38	10.52	10.52
Lv Curtis										f 3.00		f 4.40	4.40		
Lv Pine	f 12.31	f 12.31								f 3.03		4.42	4.42	f 10.56	f 10.56
Lv Buffington	12.34	12.34				7.01				3.06		4.45	4.45	11.00	11.00
Lv Gibson						A 6.28									
Lv Indiana Harbor	12.55	12.38			6.42	7.05	6.52	7.35		3.40		4.50	4.50	11.04	11.04
Lv Mahoning	12.57	12.40					6.55			3.42		4.53	4.53	11.07	11.07
Lv Whiting	1.07	12.43			f 6.47	7.12	6.57			3.47		4.58	4.58	11.11	11.11
Lv Robertsdale						7.15	7.00					f 5.01	f 5.01		
Lv East Side	1.13	12.49				7.20	7.03			3.52		5.06	5.06	11.17	11.17
Lv South Chicago	1.15	12.51			7.23	7.06				3.56		5.10	5.10	11.20	11.20
Lv 71st Street	1.21	12.57			7.28	7.11				4.02		5.17	5.17	11.26	
Lv Park Manor	1.23	12.59			7.30	7.15				4.04		5.19	5.19	11.28	
Lv Englewood	1.25	1.02	5.41	7.01	7.10	7.35	7.20	7.55	2.25	4.07	4.45	5.22	5.22	11.30	
Ar Chicago (La Salle St. Sta.)	1.40	1.15	5.55	7.15	7.25	7.50	7.35	8.10	2.40	4.23	5.00	5.35	5.35	11.43	
	AM	AM	AM	AM	AM	AM	AM	AM	PM	PM	PM	PM	PM	PM	

◆ No Baggage Carried.

f Stops on signal.

A Stops on signal Sunday.

B Stops on signal Saturday to discharge passengers.

C Stops on signal to discharge from Chicago and Englewood.

On holidays shown below, Sunday train service will be in effect—

New Year's Day
Memorial Day
Independence Day
Labor Day
Thanksgiving Day
Christmas Day

The time between 12:01 noon and 12:00 midnight is indicated by **dark face type**.

Form 219—Printed in U.S.A.—Poole Bros., Inc.—20M

The Soo Line provided overnight passenger service between Minneapolis and Chicago on trains 5 and 6. In addition to the mail and express traffic, the train included coach seating and an 8-section, restaurant-lounge car. Trains 5 and 6 operated between Minneapolis and Owen, Wisconsin, where the train was combined or split with the Chicago – Duluth overnight Laker. Soo 4-6-2, No. 2723 is technically a Wisconsin Central engine, and is shown here heading up the Minneapolis section illustrating the first three cars, an RPO-Baggage, a baggage car and a coach. The sleeper-restaurant-lounge was the last car in the consist. The Laker also handled the Ashland, Wisconsin, section between Chicago and Spencer. *Harold K. Vollrath Collection*

CHAPTER 3

OVERNIGHT LONG DISTANCE SERVICES

The overnight train services were indeed a superb way to travel, not only during the mid-twentieth century, but now in 2008 as well. Most of the overnight trains, of which there were literally hundreds of such services during the 1940s and '50s, provided sleeping car accommodations and coach seating plus a variety of food and beverage services. There were at least four different types of overnight trains during that time period. The route mileages for such trains were generally in the 400-mile to 1200-mile categories. However, believe it or not, such trains could operate with distances of only 160 miles, such as the Northern Pacific's overnight train between Duluth and St. Paul-Minneapolis.

The most common was the train with both Pullman and coach seating. One example of the consist of this type of train was three or four head-end cars, two coaches, a dining car or café lounge car, and three sleeping cars. This is only one example. There were many trains with two head-end cars, one coach and one sleeping car, or others with just one head-end car, three coaches, a dining car, lounge car and five or six sleeping cars. This type of train could be observed with all heavyweight equipment, or a combination of heavyweight and the new streamlined cars, or with only streamlined equipment. One example of the latter was the Burlington's Denver Zephyr, which also included dome coaches.

Overnight trains were, and are, a neat way to travel by accomplishing the trip without additional time spent at hotels, etc. The Twentieth Century Limited was once an All-Pullman sleeping car train between Chicago and New York City with some of the finest sleeping accommodations. The rear car was an observation lounge car with larger windows for viewing the nighttime scenery. The eastbound train is getting ready to depart from the LaSalle Street Station in Chicago in this 1963 view. *Herman Page*

There were also many examples of overnight trains which were combined or split en route to the destinations. One example was a local train that provided overnight sleeping car service between Chicago and Ashland, Wisconsin, which was the Ashland section of the Laker. The train made the local stops between Spencer and Ashland and consisted of three head-end cars, one coach and one sleeping car. The sleeping car and two of the head-end cars were switched into or out of the Chicago – Duluth Laker at Spencer.

Another type of overnight train was the All-Pullman train. There were several such trains during the 1950s, such as the Pennsylvania's Broadway Limited, the New York Central's Twentieth Century Limited, the Illinois Central's Panama Limited, and the Southern Pacific's Lark. The consists varied among the different railroads, but generally included one or two head-end cars, as many as twelve sleeping cars, and two or three dining and lounge cars.

Still another overnight train was the All-coach,

sometimes called All-Chair car trains. Often these ran as a companion train to an All-Pullman train. Two examples were the Baltimore and Ohio's Columbian, the companion to the Capitol Limited; and the Starlight, the companion to the Southern Pacific's Lark.

The fourth type of an overnight train was often, but not always, referred to as a Mail Train. In this case, most of these consists had but one or two coaches as part of train with anywhere from 10 to 25 head-end cars for the mail and express traffic. One example was the Milwaukee Road's Fast Mail between Minneapolis and Chicago with one coach, at least four Rail Post Office or combination RPO-Baggage cars plus well over a dozen head-end cars. The head-end cars, by the way, also included box express cars.

These are only a few examples of the many types of consists for overnight trains to be found throughout North America. The following photos and timetables illustrate some of the wide variety of such train services.

The Twentieth Century is pausing at Harmon, New York, in March 1963. By this time the overnight train also contained coaches with the combination of the Pacemaker, once an all-coach train. Harmon was also the location for changing power — diesel to electric for the trip into New York City. *Herman Page*

An example of the electric power is shown here leading the Twentieth Century at Harmon, New York. *Herman Page*

The Baltimore and Ohio operated a very convenient overnight train between Chicago and Washington, D. C., The Capitol Limited. This writer took advantage of the overnight schedule when having to report to the Interstate Commerce Commission during my employment in Marketing and Operations Research on the Milwaukee Road. (The official name of the department was Traffic Research.) This photo shows the combined Capitol Limited and the Columbian at the Grand Central Station in downtown Chicago. This station also served the Soo Line and the Chesapeake and Ohio Railroads. *Harold K. Vollrath Collection*

One very interesting train on the Canadian Pacific was the overnight service between Sault Ste. Marie, Ontario and Toronto. Passengers are getting ready to board No. 28 at the Soo for the run to Toronto. Note the heavyweight sleeper, the Renfrew, and the dome-coach-buffet-lounge car just ahead in this September 1955 scene. *Jim Scribbins*

The Canadian National Railway provided service between Winnipeg and Churchill, Manitoba. Train 93 has just arrived at Churchill. Passengers will have an opportunity to visit stores and restaurants as well as the Eskimo Museum during their stay in this northern community on the Hudson Bay. Train service is still available as this is being written in 2008 by VIA RAIL Canada over the Canadian National and Hudson Bay Railway. *Jim Scribbins*

The Illinois Central's overnight Panama Limited between Chicago and New Orleans was equipped with an observation car with square ends and diaphragms for mid-train operation. The IC's observation bar lounge, No. 3314, is part of the Panama Limited's consist. The Panama Limited was an All-Pullman sleeping car train. *Patrick C. Dorin*

The Chesapeake and Ohio's Sportsman had a variety of origins and destinations between the Midwest and the east coast. Services included sleeping cars and coach accommodations with dining car services for most of the routings. This view shows a seven-car consist, northbound at Pemberville, Ohio, in May 1966. *Bob Lorenz*

It is April 30, 1971, and the C&O's George Washington is leaving Toledo, Ohio, for Huntington on its last run. The George Washington once provided extensive sleeping car service between Cincinnati and Washington, D. C., as well as other connecting routes. This view is minus any sleeping cars and has just three coaches for the last run the day before Amtrak. *Bob Lorenz*

The Kansas City Southern's Southern Belle provided overnight service between Kansas City and New Orleans and Port Arthur with 14 roomette, 4 double bedroom sleeping cars. The train also included coaches, a dining car and a tavern-lounge-observation car. This view shows the last run of train No. 1 at Grandview, Missouri, on November 2, 1969. Sadly, it has but five cars in the consist for the last trip. Although it is not 100% certain, there appears to be a business car for the last car in the train. *Harold K. Vollrath Collection*

What was once a very popular train between Chicago and Ashland, Wisconsin — known as the Ashland Limited — eventually had a name change to the Northwoods Fisherman. The train often operated in two sections during the summer vacation periods, often as an All-Pullman consist and an All-coach consist. This 1962 view shows the Northwoods Fisherman arriving at Ashland with five cars: one baggage, one full Rail Post Office-Baggage car, one 16 duplex roomette-4 double bedroom sleeper and two coaches. *Dale Holm*

The C&NW's 16 duplex roomette – 4 double bedroom car is shown here in the consist of the North Woods Fisherman. This type of car provided sleeping accommodations for 24 passengers. *Dale Holm*

The Pennsylvania Railroad's overnight All-Pullman train was the Broadway Limited. The eastbound Broadway is shown here at Valparaiso, Indiana, in June 1965. *Frank Schnick*

The Admiral departed Chicago later after the Broadway Limited for its run to New York, providing both coach and sleeping accommodations. The eastbound is shown here speeding past the Hobart, Indiana, station, which was a stop for the PRR's commuter train services between Chicago and Valparaiso, Indiana. *Frank Schnick*

The Houstonian is rolling through Port Barre, Louisiana, with a seven-car consist powered by a Missouri Pacific 4-6-2, No. 6425. The Houstonian operated as trains 309 and 310 between New Orleans and Houston, a distance of 367 miles. The train included sleeping cars and coaches for passenger service. Head-end traffic was handled in a combination car and an RPO-Baggage car with a 30-foot Post Office section. The No. 6425, by the way, was built by Brooks in 1912 and is full speed ahead in this August 1948 photo. *Harold K. Vollrath Collection*

The Union Pacific-Milwaukee Road's City of Denver was an overnight train between Chicago and Denver. During the mid-1960s, the City of Denver was combined with the City of Portland with a continued overnight service. Eventually all of the "City" trains were combined including the Challenger. This view shows the City of Denver as part of the western run powered by two Milwaukee Road units, an FP-7 and an FP45 at Marion, Iowa. *Lloyd Keyser*

The All-Pullman Broadway Limited was powered by GG1s over the Philadelphia – New York City segment of the overnight Chicago – New York route. The Broadway provided virtually all types of sleeping car accommodations plus dining and lounge car services. An observation-sleeping car brought up the rear of the train. *William Raia*

The Colorado Eagle was the overnight train service between St. Louis and Denver on the Missouri Pacific. The train operated over the Denver, Rio Grande and Western between Pueblo, Colorado, and Denver. During the mid-1950s, the Colorado Eagle was equipped with two 10 roomette, 6 double bedroom cars between St. Louis and Denver, and also one 6 roomette, 6 section, 4 double bedroom car between Wichita and Denver plus coaches including a dome coach. One of the coaches was a combination grill-coach. A diner-lounge car provided the meal services for dinner and breakfast. Head-end traffic was an important part of the Colorado Eagle business. In this view, the Colorado Eagle is at Denver. Note the amount of mail, express and baggage on the carts next to the head-end cars. *William Raia*

The New York Central operated an extensive fleet of trains between the Midwest and New York into the 1960s. Table No. 2 from the April 24, 1960, schedules illustrates the fleet of eastbound trains from Chicago to New York. A similar number of trains operated from New York to Chicago.

Schedules shown on this page are in terms of "LOCAL TIME" (standard or daylight) as observed by each city. . . . On cities marked with ★ also see reference note.

CHICAGO—TOLEDO—CLEVELAND—BUFFALO—ALBANY—BOSTON and NEW YORK

Table No. 2 — EASTBOUND

	44 Ex. Sat.	208 Daily	6 Daily	16 Daily	8 Daily	28 Daily	26 Daily	68 Daily	54 Daily	2 Daily	40 Daily	90 Daily	222 Ex. Sun.	234 Sun. Only	50 Daily	96 Daily
	OPERATES VIA DETROIT See Table No. 4	GREAT LAKES		OHIO STATE LIMITED	OPERATES VIA DETROIT See Table No. 4	NEW ENGLAND STATES	TWENTIETH CENTURY LIMITED	THE COMMODORE VANDERBILT								
Lv Chicago (CST)	9 00 AM	PM	11 30 PM	PM	1 00 PM	2 30 PM	3 30 PM	3 30 PM	AM	4 25 PM	PM	9 45 PM	12 30 AM	1 45 AM	PM	PM
Lv CHICAGO (La Salle Street Station) (CDT)	10 00		12 30		2 00	3 30	4 30	4 30		5 25		10 45	1 30	2 45		
Lv Englewood (BC)	L10 35		h 12 44		h 2 14		h 4 44	h 4 44		h 5 39						
Lv Gary (N.Y.C. Station)			1 06			H 4 02	H 5 02	H 5 02		P 5 55		11 20				
Lv Porter (NCB)																
Lv La Porte			1 39									11 54	E 2 48	E 3 52		
Lv South Bend			2 05			4 31				6 49		12 20	E 3 20	E 4 26		
Lv Elkhart			2 40			4 55	H 5 53	H 6 20		7 22		1 00	4 15	5 25		
Lv Kendallville ★			3 18			5 25							5 10	6 20		
Lv Waterloo (Fort Wayne) ★ (CDT)			3 31	E 3 31		6 10				8 07			5 50	7 00		
Lv Bryan (EST)			3 53							8 29			7 15	8 25		
Lv TOLEDO			4 50			7 22	h 8 13	h 8 13		9 30		3 10	8 00	9 00		
Lv Port Clinton (LaCarne)			5 27													
Lv Sandusky (EST)			5 43									3 57	8 30	9 20		
Lv Elyria (Oberlin) (EDT)			7 20									5 30	10 30	10 55		
Lv Linndale (NCB)		G	7 45													
Ar CLEVELAND (Union Terminal)			8 00			10 12				12 20		6 20	11 30	11 55		
Lv CLEVELAND (Union Terminal)		6 15		8 25	9 45	10 27				12 45		7 15	12 30	12 55		
Lv East Cleveland		6 24		8 34								7 24	12 39	1 04		
Lv Painesville		7 02		9 12								8 05	1 16	1 40		
Lv Geneva		PP7 20											1 36	1 58		
Lv Ashtabula		7 35		9 35						2 05		8 30	1 50	2 10		
Lv Conneaut													2 10	2 25		
Lv Erie		8 25		10 20	11 18					2 48		9 10	2 45	3 00		
Lv North East																
Lv Westfield		9 05		10 50								9 40	3 20	3 25		
Lv Dunkirk		9 30		11 10								10 05	3 40	3 45		
Ar BUFFALO (Central Terminal) (EDT)	10 25	10 30		10 30	12 05	1 05				4 25		11 05	4 50	4 50		
Lv BUFFALO (Central Terminal) (EDT)	10 59			12 25	12 59	1 18	1 35			4 39	8 00	11 32			1 45	2 25
Ar Batavia	11 38			K 12 59							8 36	12 08				
Ar Rochester	12 04				T 2 02	M 2 16				5 38	9 05	12 37			2 48	3 24
Ar Newark											9 36	1 08				
Ar Lyons											9 46					
Ar Syracuse	1 24			2 40	i 3 14	3 31	L 3 51			6 53	10 33	1 57			4 01	4 39
Ar Oneida										7 24	11 04					
Ar Rome										7 41	11 21					5 23
Ar Utica	2 18			K 3 29						7 57	11 37	2 51			4 55	5 59
Ar Herkimer (Mohawk-Ilion)										8 19	11 59					
Ar Little Falls										8 31						
Ar Fort Plain										8 46		V 3 30				
Ar Amsterdam										9 18	12 55					6 48
Ar Schenectady										9 38	1 13	4 12			6 08	7 07
Ar ALBANY	4 05			5 11	G 5 09 / 5 42	5 21 / 5 59	6 08	i 6 30	i 6 30	10 19	1 51	5 00			6 35	7 50

	62 Daily	28 Daily	400 Daily	404 Daily	60 Daily
	MONTREAL LIMITED			THE MOHAWK	HUDSON RIVER SPECIAL
Lv ALBANY	AM	AM 6 20	AM 10 45	PM	PM
Ar Chatham			11 15		
Ar Pittsfield			11 47		
Ar Springfield		7 21	12 56		
Ar Palmer		8 33	1 20		
Ar Worcester		9 47	2 05		
Ar Framingham		i10 18	2 33		
Ar Newtonville		i10 56	2 50		
Ar Huntington Ave.		i11 15	3 25		
Ar BOSTON (South Station) (EDT)		11 20 AM	3 30		

(Columns 26 and 68: "All Coach Seats Reserved See Pages 20-21")

	44	6	16	8	28	54	2	40	90	222	234	50	96
Lv ALBANY	4 15	4 45	5 18	5 49	6 05		8 30	10 34	2 01	4 00	5 35	6 40	8 10
Ar Hudson		5 19					9 05		2 40	C 6 08	4 36		8 45
Ar Rhinecliff							9 30		3 06	C 6 31	5 00		9 15
Ar Poughkeepsie	5 25	C 5 59		N 7 00	N 7 17		9 50	11 44	3 29	6 45			9 40
Ar Beacon		C 6 14					10 10		3 47				10 00
Ar Peekskill	B 5 42						10 38						10 12
Ar Harmon	i 6 17	i 6 47	i 7 17	i 7 47	i 8 04		W10 52	i12 36	H 4 23 / 4 50	i 7 37		i 8 35	10 37
Ar Yonkers	i 6 44	i 7 14					i 8 32			i 6 54			i11 23
Ar 125th St (NCB)	i 7 02						i11 39			i 7 14		i 9 18	i11 40
Ar NEW YORK (Grand Central Terminal) (EDT)	7 15	7 45	8 15	8 45	9 00		9 30 / 11 50	1 35	5 25	8 35	7 25	9 35	11 55
	AM	AM	AM	AM	AM	AM	AM / PM	PM	PM	PM	PM	PM	PM

For explanation of Reference Marks, see Page 6.   For Sleeping Car, Coach and Dining Car Service, see Pages 15 to 19.

The New York Central continued for many years to include advertisements of the types of service within the timetables. This April 24, 1960, ad illustrates the Sleepercoach services between Chicago and New York and Chicago and Boston.

This set of timetables from page 26 of the Chicago and North Western April 28, 1940, shows a variety of overnight schedules (Tables 17 and 19), a long distance local between Minneapolis and Ashland, Wisconsin (Table 18), and a short distance local between Ashland and Bayfield (Table 18a). An interesting point about Table 17 is that the Soo Line overnight train between Chicago and Duluth is included because the C&NW and the Soo honored each other's tickets. Passengers had a choice of three trains each way daily, plus an additional train north on Fridays and south on Sundays.

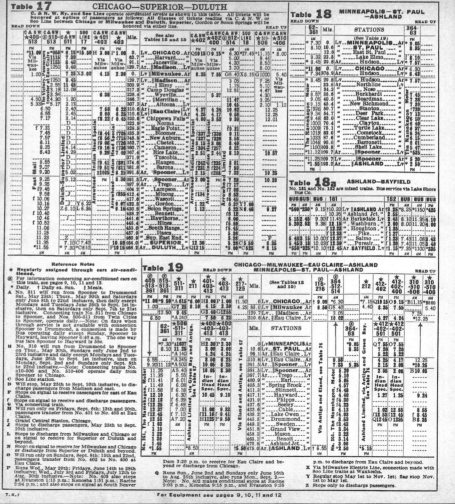

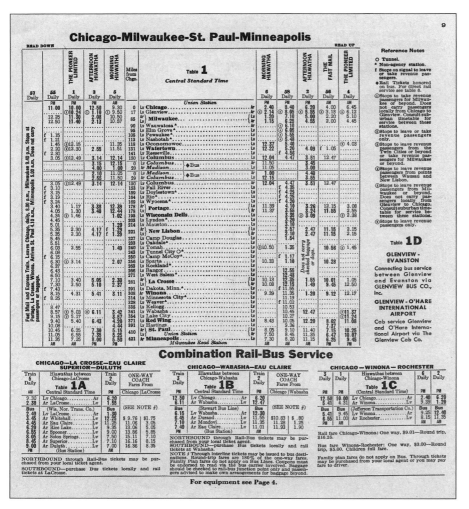

Table No.1 illustrates the extent of the Milwaukee Road passenger services between Chicago and the Twin Cities in this April 26, 1964, timetable. The Milwaukee Road operated five trains in each direction on a daily basis at that time. Now (2008) there is only one Amtrak train each way over the former Milwaukee Road between Chicago and the Twin Cities — the transcontinental Empire Builder.

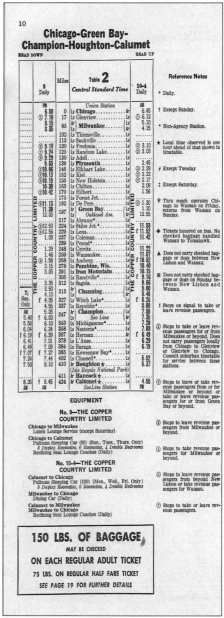

Table No. 2 illustrates the overnight Chicago – Calumet, Michigan, train over the Milwaukee Road and the Soo Line — the former Duluth, South Shore and Atlantic Railroad. The equipment listing shows the Copper Country Limited provided both sleeping car and coach accommodations. *Milwaukee Road, April 26, 1964*

The PERE MARQUETTES

STREAMLINERS — TRAINS 3 · 8

COACH ★ PARLOR CAR ★ TAVERN LOUNGE DINING CAR

CHICAGO • ST. JOSEPH • BENTON HARBOR • HOLLAND • MUSKEGON • GRAND RAPIDS

Miles	EASTBOUND—READ DOWN	8 Daily	2 Ex. Sat. Night	Resort Special Fri. Only
	(Central Time)	PM	PM	PM
0	Lv **Chicago** Grand Central Station	**4.20**	**11.15**	**8.45**
9	Lv Chicago, 63rd St. B. & O. Station	**4.40**	**11.35**	**9.04**
19	Lv South Chicago B. & O. Station	**5.00**	**11.55**	**9.24**
59	Lv Michigan City	M **5.42**		
	(Eastern Time)			
69	Lv **New Buffalo**			
80	Lv Sawyer			
84	Lv Bridgman			**The**
96	Lv **St. Joseph**	**7.21**	2.14	**Resort Special**
98	Lv **Benton Harbor**	**7.26**	2.35	**11.57**
104	Lv Riverside			Will Operate
107	Lv Coloma			Fridays Only
110	Lv Watervliet	C **7.40**	C 2.53	from Chicago
115	Lv **Hartford**	C **7.46**	C 3.00	Beginning June 22
124	Lv **Bangor**	**8.01**	3.27	Last Run from
131	Lv Grand Junction			Chicago Sept. 7
136	Lv Pullman			
138	Lv Bravo			
144	Lv Fennville	C **8.25**	C 3.51	
148	Lv New Richmond			
151	Lv East Saugatuck			
159	Ar **Holland**	**8.51**	4.10	1.20
0	Lv **Holland**	**8.56**	4.55	
10	Lv West Olive		5.14	
21	Lv Grand Haven	**9.30**	5.40	
31	Lv Muskegon Heights	f **9.46**	f 6.00	
34	Ar **Muskegon**	**9.55**	6.10	
159	Lv **Holland**	**8.51**	4.25	1.20
164	Lv Zeeland			
173	Lv Hudsonville			
178	Lv Grandville			
184	Ar **Grand Rapids**	**9.25**	5.00	2.00
332	Ar Traverse City (See page 6 for intermediate Stations)		11.22	6.30
394	Ar Charlevoix		**1.23**	8.10
409	Ar Petoskey		**1.55**	8.40
410	Ar Bay View			
	(Eastern Time)	PM	PM	AM

WESTBOUND—READ DOWN	3 Ex. Sun.	5 Sun. & Hol. ♂	7 Ex. Sat. & Sun. Night	Resort Special Sun. Only from Petoskey
(Eastern Time)	AM	PM	PM	PM
Lv Bay View (See page 6 for intermediate Stations)				
Lv Petoskey			A **4.00**	**8.00**
Lv Charlevoix			A **4.32**	**8.30**
Lv Traverse City			A **6.21**	**10.22**
Lv **Grand Rapids**	8.00	**6.30**	**11.59**	3.00
Lv Grandville				
Lv Hudsonville				
Lv Zeeland				
Ar **Holland**	8.38	**7.08**	12.58	3.30
Lv **Muskegon**	7.20	**5.40**	**11.30**	
Lv Muskegon Heights	f 7.30	f **5.50**	f **11.40**	
Lv Grand Haven	7.46	**6.06**	**11.56**	
Lv West Olive				
Ar **Holland**	8.21	**6.41**	12.30	
Lv **Holland**	8.38	**7.08**	1.13	3.30
Lv East Saugatuck				**The**
Lv New Richmond				**Resort Special**
Lv Fennville	9.01	**7.30**	E 1.36	Will Operate
Lv Bravo				Sundays Only
Lv Pullman				from Petoskey
Lv Grand Junction				Beginning June 24
Lv **Bangor**	9.25	**7.54**	2.18	ex. WILL NOT
Lv McDonald				RUN Sept. 2
Lv **Hartford**	E 9.40	E **8.08**	E 2.32	
Lv Watervliet	E 9.47	E **8.14**	E 2.38	
Lv Coloma				
Lv **Benton Harbor**	10.05	**8.32**	3.22	5.09
Lv **St. Joseph**	10.10	**8.38**	3.28	but WILL RUN
Lv Stevensville				Sept. 3
Lv Bridgman				Leaves
Lv Sawyer				Grand Rapids
Lv **New Buffalo**				following day
(Central Time)				Last run from
Lv Michigan City	N 9.50	N **8.16**		Petoskey Sept. 9
Lv South Chicago B. & O. Station	10.29	**8.56**	4.05	5.41
Lv Chicago, 63rd St. B. & O. Station	10.48	**9.15**	4.30	6.05
Ar **Chicago** Grand Central Station	11.10	**9.40**	5.00	6.30
(Central Time)	AM	PM	AM	AM

TRAIN NO. 2—Daily except Saturday night
Sleepers ready at 9:00 p.m., C.T. may be occupied at Grand Rapids and Muskegon until 8:00 a.m., E.T.
Sleeping Cars—
Chicago to Grand Rapids—
10 Roomettes, 6 Dbl. Bedrooms (Car 21.)
Chicago to Muskegon—
10 Roomettes, 6 Dbl. Bedrooms. (Car 202.)
Chicago to Petoskey
10 Roomettes, 6 Dbl. Bedrooms. (Car 22)
Sunday to Thursday inclusive
First trip Monday, June 25.
Last run Thursday, September 6.
Will not operate Monday, Sept. 3.
Coaches.

TRAIN NO. 8—Daily—Streamlined
Chicago to Grand Rapids
Parlor Car (Car 81) Railroad Owned.
Coaches—
Tavern Diner—Dining, tavern and snack service

THE RESORT SPECIAL
Sleeping Cars—
Chicago to Petoskey
2—10 Roomettes, 6 Dbl. Bedrooms. (Cars 101-2)
6 Single Bedrooms, Tavern-Lounge (Car 103)
Chicago to Traverse City
10 Roomettes, 6 Dbl. Bedrooms. (Car 104).
May be occupied until 8.00 am.
Chicago to Petoskey
Coaches.

REFERENCE NOTES

C—Stops on flag to let off pay passengers only from South Chicago, 63rd Street and Grand Central Station, Chicago. Will also stop on flag to pick up pay passengers only for Holland, Grand Rapids or Muskegon and beyond.

f—Stops on flag to pick up passengers or on request to let off passengers.

M—Stops on signal to receive passengers for Holland and points beyond.

Page 2

TRAIN NO. 7—Daily except Saturday and Sunday
Sleepers ready at Grand Rapids and Muskegon 9:30 p.m., E.T., may be occupied at Chicago until 8.00 a.m., C.T.
Sleeping Cars—
Grand Rapids to Chicago—(Car 71.)
10 Roomettes, 6 Dbl. Bedrooms
Muskegon to Chicago—(Car 281.)
10 Roomettes, 6 Dbl. Bedrooms.
Petoskey to Chicago—(Car 160.)
10 Roomettes, 6 Dbl. Bedrooms.
Monday to Friday inclusive.
First trip Tuesday, June 26.
Last run Friday, September 7.
Will not operate Monday, September 3 and Tuesday, September 4.
Coaches.

TRAIN NO. 5—Sunday and Holidays
Pullman Sleeper as Parlor Car
10 Roomettes, 6 Bedrooms
From Grand Rapids .... Car 51

THE RESORT SPECIAL
Sleeping Cars—
Petoskey to Chicago
2—10 Roomettes, 6 Dbl. Bedrooms. (Cars 111-2)
Traverse City to Chicago
10 Roomette, 6 Dbl. Bdrms. (Car 114)
Ready at Traverse City 10 p.m.
Petoskey to Chicago
6 Single Bedrooms, Tavern-Lounge (Car 113)
Coaches—

REFERENCE NOTES

♂—Runs Sundays, also on the following Holidays, Memorial Day May 30, July 4 and Labor Day September 3.

A—Daily, except Sunday. Makes no connection at Grand Rapids on Saturdays as train No. 7 does not operate out of

This Pere Marquette Time Table from May 20, 1951, page 2, illustrates the afternoon and morning operations between Chicago and Grand Rapids, Michigan, plus the overnight sleeping car services to Muskegon and Petoskey. The Muskegon sleeping car assignments were among the shortest runs in North America. The table also shows the Resort Special for weekend trips between Chicago and Petoskey.

14

PITTSBURGH TO BALTIMORE, WASHINGTON, PHILADELPHIA AND NEW YORK

Table 8 — Eastern Standard Time

Miles		The Admiral 50 Daily	Pennsylvania Limited 54 Daily	⊕ The Duquesne 16 Except Sat.	⊕ The Duquesne 12 Sat. only	⊕ The Juniata 24 Except Sat.	Manhattan Limited 22 Daily	22-48 Except Sat. & Mar. 24	The Penn Texas / Cincinnati Limited 4 Daily	The General 48 Daily	"Spirit of St. Louis" 30 Daily	Broadway Limited 28 Daily
		AM	AM N. B.	PM	PM	PM	PM	PM	PM	AM	AM	AM N. B.
.0	Lv **PITTSBURGH, Pa.**	5.15	9.10	12.55	1.55	4.00	10.00	10.00	11.47	12.11	12.58	1.34
6.6	" Wilkinsburg	------	9.26	------	------	4.16	10.16	10.16	------	------	------	All Private
30.8	" Greensburg	5.54	9.52	1.34	2.34	4.45	10.45	10.45	------	------	------	Room
40.1	" Latrobe	------	10.05	1.47	2.47	4.58	10.58	10.58	------	------	------	Train
76.4	" Johnstown	6.48	10.45	2.29	3.29	5.40	11.40	11.40	------	------	------	
113.9	" Altoona-(♦)	7.50	11.49	3.25	4.25	6.45	12.45	12.45	2.09	2.45	3.40	4.03
128.1	" Tyrone-(♦)	8.14	------	3.45	4.46	7.11	------	------	------	------	------	------
147.7	" Huntingdon	8.42	------	4.12	5.12	7.38	------	------	------	------	------	------
159.6	" Mount Union	------	------	------	------	f 7.52	------	------	------	------	------	------
184.1	" Lewistown (Penna. State University-♦)	9.18	1.07	4.48	5.47	8.18	2.09	2.09	------	------	------	------
244.7	Ar **Harrisburg**	10.24	2.13	5.55	6.55	9.26	3.15	3.15	4.29	5.05	5.56	d 6.19
244.7	Lv **Harrisburg**	------	▲2.40	▲6.00	------	------	♦5.40	------	♦5.40	5.40	------	------
271.8	Ar York, Pa.	------	▲3.26	▲6.55	------	------	♦6.30	------	♦6.30	6.30	------	------
328.0	" **Baltimore, Md.** (Penna. Station)	------	▲5.05	▲8.45	------	------	♦8.10	------	♦8.10	8.10	------	------
368.1	Ar **WASHINGTON, D. C.**	------	▲6.50	▲9.35	------	------	♦9.15	------	♦9.15	9.15	------	------
244.7	Lv **Harrisburg, Pa.**	10.40	2.13	5.55	6.55	9.40	3.35	5.30	4.29	5.30	5.56	d 6.19
280.0	" Lancaster	11.13	2.56	6.36	7.36	10.12	4.08	6.03	------	6.03	6.37	------
309.3	" Coatesville	§11.40	3.25	7.02	8.02	------	------	------	------	------	------	------
327.9	" Paoli	12.00	3.45	7.22	8.22	10.58	d 4.55	d 6.48	d 5.56	d 6.48	7.24	d 7.36
------	Ar **Philadelphia** **Penna. Station** (30th St.)	------	------	------	------	11.30	d 5.30	------	------	------	------	------
	Connecting Train No. →					160						
------	Lv **Penna. Station** (30th St.)	------	------	------	------	11.40	------	------	------	------	------	------
353.4	Ar **North Philadelphia Station**	d12.40	4.15	7.53	8.53	------	------	d 7.20	d 6.25	d 7.20	d 7.52	d 8.03
381.2	" Trenton, N. J.	d 1.23	4.43	8.24	9.25	12.20	6.36	d 7.52	d 7.05	d 7.52	------	------
429.3	Ar **Newark**	d 2.11	5.30	d 9.09	10.10	1.09	d 7.31	d 8.39	d 7.52	d 8.39	d 9.05	d 9.15
------	Lv Newark	2.21	5.32	x 9.12	10.21	1.30	7.36	p 8.45	y 7.57	r 8.45	9.06	9.21
------	Ar Jersey City (Exchange Place) (u)	2.38	5.49	x 9.28	10.37	1.46	7.58	p 9.02	y 8.14	r 9.02	9.28	9.38
------	" New York (Hudson Terminal) (u)	2.41	5.52	x 9.31	10.40	1.49	8.01	p 9.05	y 8.17	r 9.05	9.31	9.41
439.3	Ar **NEW YORK, N. Y.** (Penna. Station)	2.50	5.45	9.25	10.25	1.35	7.55	8.55	8.15	8.55	9.20	9.30
		PM	PM	PM	PM	AM	AM	AM	AM	AM	AM	AM

Sleeping Cars and Reserved Seat Coaches. For Special Service Charge in Coaches See Page 3

CAR SERVICE—(Table 8)
Regularly Assigned Cars Are Air-Conditioned

No. 4—Sleeping Cars, Dining Car and Reclining Seat Coaches to New York.
Coaches, Harrisburg to Washington.
Snack Bar Coach Harrisburg to Washington. (Hot-Cold Food and Beverages).

No. 12—Coaches. Snack Bar Coach Hot-Cold Food and Beverages.

No. 16—Coaches. Snack Bar Coach Hot-Cold Food and Beverages.

No. 22—Through sleeping car enroute from Chicago to New York.
Sleeping Cars......Pittsburgh to New York (12 Duplex Rooms, 4 Double Bedrooms).
Pittsburgh to New York (10 Roomettes, 6 Double Bedrooms) (Except Saturdays and Mar. 24) (*To No. 48 at Harrisburg*). (*Sleeping Cars open for occupancy in Pittsburgh 9.00 p.m.*)
Snack Bar Coach..................Harrisburg to Washington (Hot-Cold Food and Beverages).
Reclining Seat Coaches......Pittsburgh to New York. Harrisburg to Washington.

No. 22-48—Sleeping Car...Pittsburgh to New York (10 Roomettes, 6 Double Bedrooms) (Except Saturdays and Mar. 24). (*Sleeping Car open in Pittsburgh 9.00 p.m.*).
Dining Car and Lounge Coach Bar Harrisburg to New York.

No. 24—Coaches.

No. 28—Sleeping, Bar Lounge Observation and Dining Cars to New York. *No Coaches or Checked Baggage.*

No. 30—Sleeping Cars, Bar Lounge Car, Dining Car and Reclining Seat Coaches.

No. 48—Sleeping, Bar Lounge and Dining Cars, Reserved Seat Coaches and Lounge Coach (Bar)—Coach attendant Service to New York. Sleeping Car and Reserved Seat Coaches—Coach Attendant Service to Washington.
For Special Service Charge in Reserved Seat Coaches, see Page 3.
Snack Bar Coach Harrisburg to Washington—Hot-Cold Food and Beverages.

No. 50—Sleeping Car, Snack Bar Coach (Hot-Cold Food and Beverages) and Reclining Seat Coaches.

No. 54—Sleeping Cars, Snack Bar Coach (Hot-Cold Food and Beverages) and Reclining Seat Coaches to New York. Coaches Harrisburg to Baltimore and Baltimore to Washington.

Reference Marks

§ Sundays only.

⊕ Coaches only; no dining car or parlor car service.

♦ Connecting train. Passengers change trains at Harrisburg.

▲ Connecting train. Passengers change trains at Harrisburg and Baltimore.

♦ Bus service is operated on limited schedule between Lewistown and Pennsylvania State University, also between Altoona, Tyrone and Pennsylvania State University by Fullington Auto Bus Company. Through tickets may be purchased from Pennsylvania Railroad agents when routed via Lewistown and baggage may be checked to State College, Pa.

N.B.—No checked baggage handled on this train.

d Stops only to discharge passengers.

f Stops only on signal or notice to agent or conductor to receive or discharge passengers.

p On Saturdays operates 6 minutes later.

r On Saturdays and Sundays operates 6 minutes later.

u Port Authority Trans-Hudson Station.

x On Sundays operates 9 minutes later.

y On Saturdays and Sundays operates 9 minutes later.

Go places together . . . at worthwhile savings! Ask about Pennsy Family Fares.

It is slightly more than four years to the dawn of Amtrak, but in 1967, the Pennsylvania Railroad still operated ten trains daily in each direction between New York City and Pittsburgh. Most of the trains operated to and from St. Louis and Chicago. Note the car service listings for equipment on the various trains below the schedule. *Pennsylvania Railroad, January 26, 1967, p. 14.*

Daytime services between Chicago and St. Louis were provided by the Wabash Railroad, as well as the Gulf, Mobile and Ohio and the Illinois Central. It is December 1947, and the streamlined equipment is under consideration and in the process of being ordered. The Wabash Blue Bird is rolling along at high speed with the streamlined Hudson (4-6-4) with a six-car consist with a combine on the head-end, coaches, dining car and a parlor observation. *Harold K. Vollrath Collection*

CHAPTER 4

LONG DISTANCE DAY TRAINS

The long distance day train service covers a great deal of territory. Many of these trains evolved into high-speed streamliner service beginning in the 1930s. Again there were hundreds of such daytime schedules across North America. Here are a just a few examples of the many routes:

Chicago – Twin Cities
Chicago – St. Louis
New York – Buffalo
Boston – Washington (as part of the Northeast corridor)
San Francisco – Los Angeles
Portland – Oakland / San Francisco
Chicago – Detroit
Chicago – Ashland, Wisconsin
New York – Pittsburgh
New York – Montreal
Chicago – Toronto
Spokane – Seattle

The equipment consists for these types of train varied depending upon the type of service, which is common for all types of train services. The Twin Cities Zephyrs were equipped with dome coaches plus parlor car seating and food and beverage services. Most of the Milwaukee Road Hiawathas and the C&NW 400s were day schedules with coach and parlor car accommodations and a variety of food and beverage service equipment.

An example of a Twin Cities Hiawatha included one RPO-baggage car, several coaches, a Super Dome lounge car, a dining car, a parlor car and a parlor Skytop observation lounge car. The Flambeau 400's summer consist included one RPO-baggage car, a Baggage Tap Café lounge car, two coaches and one parlor car. The winter consist was reduced to one RPO-baggage, one coach-lounge car and one coach.

Some day trains had but one coach for passengers and handled up to a dozen head-end cars for mail and express traffic. The Milwaukee Road operated one such train on a daily basis from Minneapolis to Chicago.

The Southern Pacific operated a fleet of Daylights on the West Coast. The fleet was equipped with both coach and parlor car seating plus food and beverage cars. There was the Shasta Daylight between Portland and Oakland, and the Coast Daylight between San Francisco and Los Angeles. These were fast streamliners that provided an opportunity for travel and viewing the beautiful scenery of Oregon and California.

Other examples of neat daytime services were the C&O's Pere Marquettes between Chicago and Grand Rapids, Michigan, and the set between Grand Rapids and Detroit. These trains were equipped with coaches as well as at least one head-end car and food and beverage service.

It can be said that the daytime train service is still a superb method of travel, offering a chance to relax, meet new friends and see parts of North America.

The Gulf, Mobile and Ohio once advertised "6 trains Each Way Chicago-St. Louis." Train No. 1, The Limited, to St. Louis was equipped with coaches, parlor car with drawing room and a dining lounge car plus heavy head-end traffic. The train departed Chicago in the late morning with St. Louis arrival in the afternoon before supper. No. 1 is shown here at Joliet crossing the Rock Island tracks. *Jim Scribbins, William Raia Collection, March 10, 1967*

The Cincinnatian was often powered with streamlined steam power, such as 5304 leading train No. 53 with seven cars near Dressler, Ohio, in May 1953. *Harold K. Vollrath Collection*

The Baltimore and Ohio's Cincinnatian was an all-coach train between Cincinnati and Detroit. No. 54 is shown here at Deshler, Ohio, in July 1956. The train was equipped with reclining seat coaches, a Fiesta car and an observation lounge diner. The train operated on an approximate six-hour schedule in both directions during the 1950s over the 259-mile route. *Harold K. Vollrath Collection*

B&O's trains 245 and 246 provided a daytime service between Wheeling and Newark, Ohio, a distance of 108.8 miles. The running time was 3 hours, 12 minutes to Newark, and 4 hours, 15 minutes to Wheeling. The train had an important mail contract. Therefore the consist included a 60-foot Rail Post Office car with a full mail section. This photo shows train 246 near Cambridge, Ohio, in August 1956. *Harold K. Vollrath Collection*

The B&O went in big for the Rail Diesel Cars. A very refreshing coach service was provided between Pittsburgh and Philadelphia with a modified RDC-2 as a baggage-diner-coach, plus two RDC-1 coaches. The scheduled running time for the RDC assignment was about 8 hours, 30 minutes for the 435-mile distance. The lead car is shown here at Pittsburgh in April 1968. *Harold K. Vollrath Collection*

Gas-electric cars were center stage for self-propelled equipment prior to the RDCs. In this view, the Gulf, Mobile and Ohio's train No. 9 operated from Bloomington, Illinois, over the former Alton's route on the Kansas City line. The rear of this motor car once had coach accommodations, while the trailer was a combination RPO-coach. The coach section had large rear windows with facing seats and an open platform — observation style. The train is shown here at the Jacksonville, Illinois, stop in April 1959. *Jim Scribbins*

Southern Pacific's train No. 52, the San Joaquin Daylight with the 4-8-4, No. 4481 is taking on water during a stop at Livingston, California, in March 1955. Livingston was not a scheduled stop for passengers during the 1950s. The train is equipped with streamlined chair cars as well as a coffee shop car and a tavern car. The Daylight operated between Oakland and Los Angeles as trains 51 northbound and 52 southbound. The train also handled the through equipment for the Sacramento. Trains 51 and 52 were scheduled for 12 hours each way over the 482-mile route, which included the connection between the Oakland Pier and San Francisco. This segment took about 30 minutes. *W. C. Whittaker*

A bit of history about the SP Daylights — the first Daylight was placed in service by the SP in 1922. The train was re-equipped in 1930 and became the West Coast's first streamlined train in 1936. From that time until the late 1950s, the trains consisted of chair cars, coffee shop, diner, tavern and parlor cars. In the late 1950s and early 1960s, the dome lounge cars replaced the tavern cars on various runs. However, the dome cars did not operate on the Coast Daylight on a permanent basis. This photo shows train No. 98 (The Coast Daylight) with the Stream-lined Steam No. 4410 at full speed en route to Los Angeles. Train 98 was scheduled for a 9-hour, 45-minute run for the 470 miles between San Francisco and Los Angeles. *Harold K. Vollrath Collection*

The Missouri Pacific operated a fast daytime train service between Omaha, Kansas City and St. Louis, a distance of 478 miles. Train services included coaches, a parlor car and dining and lounge facilities. The train was known as the Missouri River Eagle. The Eagle is shown here at Atkinson, Kansas, in November 1947 with its six-car consist. Note the porthole windows on the diesel. *Harold K. Vollrath Collection*

The Northwestern Pacific (a subsidiary of the Southern Pacific) operated a day train service, trains 3 and 4, between San Rafael and Eureka, California, 267 miles. A Greyhound Bus service provided the connection between San Francisco and San Rafael, a distance of 17 miles. Train No. 3 was scheduled for 9 hours, 30 minutes to San Rafael, while No. 4 to Eureka covered the route in 9 hours, 35 minutes. The train was known as the Redwood, and No. 4 is shown here north of Spyrock, California, in February 1957. The two-car train was powered by an SD-7 or 9. The baggage car also contained a coffee maker and the attendant had enough sandwiches and pastry to keep the passengers from getting hungry. *Both Photos, Jim Scribbins*

The Flying Yankee was built in late 1934, and went into service between Portland and Bangor, Maine, in 1935. The train served on that route for a number of years and then was transferred to other routes such as Boston to New Bethlehem, New Hampshire, and Boston to White River Junction. The three-unit articulated streamliner included coach seating as well as a buffet plus a lounge observation room. The Flying Yankee was a joint venture between the Boston and Maine and the Maine Central. The Flying Yankee is shown here at Boston in July 1941. *Harold K. Vollrath Collection*

It is October 1965, and the Wabash Railroad has been absorbed into the Norfolk and Western. The N&W's train No. 111 is the St. Louis bound Banner Blue that just cleared the 21st Street crossing in Chicago. The train's consist includes a dome coach, and a dome solarium-parlor, both from the streamlined Blue Bird. The remaining cars include one baggage car, one chair car and one food-beverage car. *Jim Scribbins*

The Illinois Central was also a prominent passenger train operator between Chicago and St. Louis. The Green Diamond, No. 21, is shown here en route to St. Louis as it races along the electrified commuter rail trains to the left of the train in this May 1942 photo. The Green Diamond operated as trains 21 and 22 and provided a daytime service. In the mid-1950s, the Green Diamond was equipped with a parlor observation car, a parlor tavern-lounge car, a diner, a tavern coach and delux reclining seat chair cars. The running time between Chicago and St. Louis, 294.2 miles, was 5 hours, 30 minutes in both directions for 21 and 22. The IC also operated the Daylight between Chicago and St. Louis with a similar schedule. The overnight train was called the Night Diamond. *Harold K. Vollrath Collection*

The Wabash Railroad's City of Kansas City, train No. 3, is shown here en route from St. Louis to Kansas City. The 278-mile route was covered in 5 hours, 20 minutes to Kansas City, and 5 hours, 40 minutes for No. 12 to St. Louis. The six-car train was designated a "Domeliner" with its dome chair car. Other equipment included two head-end cars, a dining car, and a Coffee Shop Club for coach passengers. Four of the six cars were heavyweight cars for this particular consist during the summer of 1960. Note the Alco PA diesel units with the original Wabash color scheme of blue and white, and then the later scheme of blue and gold striping and lettering. *William S. Kuba*

Chicago and North Western's Flambeau 400 operated between Ashland, Wisconsin, and Chicago. Beginning in the late 1950s, the Flambeau and the Peninsula 400 (Chicago – Ishpeming, Michigan) were equipped with bi-level coaches. The eastbound Flambeau is shown here at Saxon, Wisconsin, (between Ashland and Ironwood, Michigan) with a neat 5-car consist. The RPO-baggage has a 15-foot Rail Post Office section. The last two cars include one single level "400" coach and one coach-lounge car in the UP colors. The Flambeau was a very popular summer and winter-ski-season train. *August 24, 1959, D. Christiansen, William Raia Collection*

Chicago and North Western's train No. 13 was a day train between Chicago and Omaha with a schedule of 12 hours, 15 minutes for the 488-mile run. The "City" Streamliners ran the route in less than 8 hours. The consist of No. 13 included three coaches with four head-end cars. The train is shown here at Norway, Iowa, in March 1954. *Lloyd Keyser*

It is 1969, and passenger services are coming close to being history on many routes throughout the United States. However, the Chicago – Detroit route did survive. Here is a five-car train en route from Detroit to Chicago on the Penn Central at Jackson, Michigan. *Patrick C. Dorin*

It is April 1962 and the eastbound Kate Shelly 400 is departing Dixon, Illinois, en route to Chicago. Since 1957, the train had been cut back from its Cedar Rapids, Iowa, to Chicago to a Clinton, Iowa, to the Windy City until discontinued with the advent of Amtrak in 1971. The Kate Shelly continued to have a full dining car until 1967. *Mark Llanuza*

The Rock Island chose not to join Amtrak, and continued operating passenger trains between Chicago and Peoria. The train, once known as the Peorian, operated east to Chicago in the morning, and returned to Peoria in the evening. In 1969, it made the trip in a little over three hours for the 161-mile run. At that time, the train was also equipped with chair cars, a parlor car and a club-diner. The train is shown here laying over at night. *Mark Llanuza*

When one thinks of mixed trains, the thought generally comes up with a picture of a local freight train operating over a branch line with a few freight cars and one combination baggage-coach, or possibly one baggage car and one coach. This is a rare photo of a Union Pacific train (Possibly No. 117), which operated between Kansas City and Denver as a mixed train with both freight and passenger power on the head-end — note the consist — with the piggyback cars following the coach. It is April 1971 and Amtrak is about three weeks away. *Harold K. Vollrath Collection*

This view shows a Chicago and Eastern Illinois Railroad Passenger Extra on the south side of Chicago. Baggage cars were also operated on special passenger trains to handle luggage or equipment, such as golf carts or skis and many other items. The cars were also operated for a food service bar, and for many activities such as dancing. One person told this writer that he danced the entire distance on a Square Dance Special on the Milwaukee Road between Chicago and St. Paul. The first two cars in this C&EI extra are baggage cars and the next three are coaches for the special run. The complete consist, which required two E-7 units, is not known. However, this Special is one more example of the type of train services that can be provided for North America. *William Raia*

The identity of this train is not exactly known, but it is one of the Pere Marquettes, most likely operating between Chicago and Grand Rapids, Michigan. The train is shown here at the older Grand Rapids Station, which was eventually replaced with a new depot to the west of downtown Grand Rapids. Why was the station demolished? So a highway could be constructed through the city, which in turn also destroyed many other businesses and residences. However, that was the "thinking" for North America since the 1940s. This photo was taken in August 1950. The diesel power is lettered for the Pere Marquette, which was absorbed into the C&O. The consist of the train includes one RPO-baggage, one baggage car, and eleven additional cars. At least one of the cars would be a parlor car plus a tavern-diner for food and beverage service. *William Raia*

MAJOR LEAGUE BASEBALL

BASEBALL SCHEDULE 1962

WHITE SOX
1962 HOME GAMES AT COMISKEY PARK

April 10, 12	LOS ANGELES
April 20(N), 21(LD), 22(2)	KANSAS CITY
April 27(N), 28(LD), 29(2)	BOSTON
May 1(N), 2(N), 3(N)	NEW YORK
May 15(N), 16(N)	WASHINGTON
May 18(N), 19, 20(2)	BALTIMORE
May 21(N)	DETROIT
May 23(N)	CLEVELAND
May 25(N), 26(LD), 27(2)	MINNESOTA
June 15(N), 16(LD), 17(2)	LOS ANGELES
June 19(N), 20(N), 21(N)	MINNESOTA
June 22(N), 23, 24(2)	KANSAS CITY
June 29(N), 30(LD)	CLEVELAND
July 1(2)	CLEVELAND
July 4(2), 5(N)	BALTIMORE
July 12(N), 13(N), 14, 15	DETROIT
July 17(N)(2), 18(N)	WASHINGTON
Aug. 1(N)(LD), 2	BOSTON
Aug. 3, 4, 5	NEW YORK
Aug. 6(N), 7	BALTIMORE
Aug. 8(N)(2), 9(LD)	LOS ANGELES
Aug. 17(N), 18(LD), 19(2)	DETROIT
Aug. 28(N), 29(N)	MINNESOTA
Sept. 3(2), 4(N), 5(N)	CLEVELAND
Sept. 7(N), 8(LD), 9(2)	WASHINGTON
Sept. 10(N)	KANSAS CITY
Sept. 18(N), 19(N), 20(LD)	BOSTON
Sept. 21(N), 22, 23	NEW YORK

CUBS
1962 HOME GAMES AT WRIGLEY FIELD

April 13, 14, 15	ST. LOUIS
April 16, 17	PITTSBURGH
April 18, 19	HOUSTON
April 24, 25, 26	LOS ANGELES
May 4, 5, 6	SAN FRANCISCO
May 8, 9, 10	NEW YORK
May 11, 12, 13(2)	PHILADELPHIA
May 28, 29	MILWAUKEE
May 30, 31	HOUSTON
June 1, 2, 3	CINCINNATI
June 5, 6, 7	SAN FRANCISCO
June 8, 9, 10	NEW YORK
June 11(LD), 12, 13, 14	PITTSBURGH
June 25(LD), 26, 27, 28	ST. LOUIS
July 6, 7, 8(2)	MILWAUKEE
July 12(LD), 13, 14	CINCINNATI
July 20, 21, 22	LOS ANGELES
July 23(LD), 24, 25	PHILADELPHIA
July 27, 28, 29	HOUSTON
Aug. 10, 11, 12	PITTSBURGH
Aug. 14(LD), 15, 16	SAN FRANCISCO
Aug. 21, 22, 23	CINCINNATI
Aug. 24, 25, 26	MILWAUKEE
Sept. 1, 2	HOUSTON
Sept. 14, 15, 16	LOS ANGELES
Sept. 17, 18	ST. LOUIS
Sept. 26, 27	PHILADELPHIA
Sept. 28, 29, 30	NEW YORK

(2) Double Header (N) Night Game (LD) Ladies' Day
May 14—CUBS vs. WHITE SOX

July 10—All Star Game at Washington, D. C.
July 30—All Star Game at Wrigley Field, Chicago

GET UP A PARTY — ENJOY BIG LEAGUE BASEBALL IN CHICAGO! CONSULT OUR TRAVEL SPECIALISTS FOR SPECIAL GROUP ARRANGEMENTS. LOW FAMILY FARES MONDAY THROUGH THURSDAY.

1962 FOOTBALL SCHEDULE

UNIVERSITY OF MINNESOTA
HOME GAMES

Sept. 29	University of Missouri
Oct. 6	U.S. Naval Academy
Oct. 13	Northwestern University
Oct. 20	University of Illinois
Nov. 10	University of Iowa
Nov. 17	Purdue University

AWAY GAMES

Oct. 27	University of Michigan
Nov. 3	Michigan State Univ.
Nov. 24	University of Wisconsin

Public Season Ticket sale
opens July 1, 1962.
Single Game Ticket sale
opens August 1, 1962.

VIKINGS
HOME GAMES

Sept. 23	Baltimore
Oct. 7	Chicago
Oct. 14	Green Bay
Oct. 28	Philadelphia
Nov. 18	Detroit
Nov. 25	Los Angeles
Dec. 2	San Francisco

AWAY GAMES

Sept. 16	Green Bay
Sept. 30	San Francisco
Oct. 21	Los Angeles
Nov. 4	Pittsburgh
Nov. 11	Chicago
Dec. 9	Detroit
Dec. 16	Baltimore

FOOTBALL SPECIALS

To Ann Arbor - Lansing - Madison. DECIDE NOW! Make your plans to attend an out-of-town U of M football game — Get up a party.

CONSULT SPORTS TRAVEL DEPT.

THE MILWAUKEE ROAD

MINNEAPOLIS	SAINT PAUL
707 Marquette Ave.	354 Cedar St.
John Guzy, Gen. Agt.	Joe Griller, Gen. Agt.

Spring and Summer
Schedules

EFFECTIVE
APRIL 29, 1962
(Central Standard Time)

- VIA -

THE MILWAUKEE ROAD

Route of the -

SPEEDLINER FLEET
- of -
SUPER DOME HIAWATHAS
- and -
DISTINCTIVE PIONEER LIMITED
America's Finest Overnight Train

DAYLIGHT SAVINGS TIME		
Minnesota - May 27	-	Sept. 4
Wisconsin - April 29	-	Sept. 30
Illinois - April 29	-	Oct. 28

The Milwaukee Road's "Spring and Summer Schedules" (April 29, 1962) is an example of the positive atmosphere for passenger service on many railroads. This brochure not only displays the Hiawathas and Pioneer Limited, but also the daytime passenger extras for the various baseball and football game schedules in Chicago and the Twin Cities.

Effective April 29, 1962 -- Central Standard Time

- READ DOWN -   -READ UP -

The Pioneer Limited	Afternoon Hiawatha	Morning Hiawatha					Morning Hiawatha	Afternoon Hiawatha	The Pioneer Limited
9:45 PM	11:30 AM	7:45 AM	LV.	MINNEAPOLIS	AR.		5:50 PM	8:05 PM	7:25 AM
10:25 PM	11:55 AM	8:20 AM	LV.	SAINT PAUL	AR.		5:15 PM	7:35 PM	6:35 AM
11:08 PM	12:32 PM	8:58 AM	LV.	RED WING	LV.		4:20 PM	6:49 PM	5:34 AM
12:15 AM	1:26 PM	9:54 AM	LV.	WINONA	LV.		3:12 PM	5:53 PM	4:27 AM
1:05 AM	2:00 PM	10:28 AM	LV.	LA CROSSE	LV.		2:40 PM	5:24 PM	3:50 AM
	3:52 PM	12:19 PM	AR.	* COLUMBUS	LV.		12:10 PM	3:25 PM	
	4:40 PM	1:05 PM	AR.	Bus. MADISON	LV. Bus		11:15 AM	2:30 PM	
4:45 AM	4:55 PM	1:30 PM	AR.	MILWAUKEE	LV.		10:57 AM	2:23 PM	11:40 PM
6:12 AM	5:55 PM	2:29 PM	AR.	+ GLENVIEW	LV.		9:50 AM	1:20 PM	10:24 PM
6:45 AM	6:20 PM	2:55 PM	AR.	CHICAGO	LV.		9:30 AM	1:00 PM	10:00 PM

* The Hiawathas, connecting at Columbus with Greyhound air-conditioned bus, provide excellent service to and from Madison. Rail tickets are honored on bus which departs and arrives railroad stations at Columbus and Madison.

+Glenview station serves the suburbs of North and West Chicago and North Shore points.
Equipment of Hiawathas include Luxury Lounge coaches - Dining Car - Super Dome car with Cafe Lounge and Sky-top Lounge, Drawing Room Parlor Car.

The Pioneer Limited, distinctive all-room train, offers latest type Duplex and Standard Roomettes, Bedrooms, single, double and ensuite. Pullman cars between Saint Paul and Chicago and Minneapolis and Milwaukee do not operate Saturdays. Consult ticket agent for occupancy time at Minneapolis-St. Paul-Milwaukee-Chicago.

Reclining seat lounge coaches.

Buffet service and beverages, before retiring - breakfast before arrival, Club, A-la-Carte and Continental.

BASEBALL SPECIALS

7:30 AM	2:40 PM	LV.	LA CROSSE	AR.	9:45 PM	12:50 AM
8:15 AM	3:12 PM	LV.	WINONA	AR.	9:09 PM	12:15 AM
9:01 AM	3:43 PM	LV.	WABASHA	AR.		11:37 PM
9:20 AM	3:58 PM	LV.	LAKE CITY	AR.		11:24 PM
9:44 AM	4:20 PM	LV.	RED WING	AR.	8:02 PM	11:08 PM
10:08 AM	4:41 PM	LV.	HASTINGS	AR.	7:37 PM	
10:45 AM	5:15 PM	AR.	ST. PAUL	LV.	7:15 PM	10:25 PM
11:35 AM	5:50 PM	AR.	MINNEAPOLIS	LV.	6:30 PM	9:45 PM

FAST MAIL

Departs Minneapolis, 6:30 PM, St. Paul, 7:15 PM for Hastings, Red Wing, Winona, LaCrosse, Milwaukee and arrives Chicago 4:00 AM -

DAY LOCAL

Departs Minneapolis, 8:20 AM, St. Paul, 9:10 AM for all points intermediate, — arriving Milwaukee at 6:25 PM and Chicago, 8:40 PM -

Baseball Travel Bargains
— To All —
Minnesota Twins Home Games

* *

Round trip fares to Saint Paul and Minneapolis cut 30% - less than 2¢ per mile for carfree - safe - dependable and comfortable transportation. Be smart - let the engineer do the driving. Special express buses from

Round Trip — From —	
LaCrosse	$5.10
Winona	3.95
Wabasha	2.70
Lake City	2.20
Red Wing	1.60
(add 10% transportation tax)	

Saint Paul Union Station every 10 minutes direct to Metropolitan Stadium. From Minneapolis from 2nd Ave. So. & Washington (1 block from Milwaukee Road Station) every 5 minutes. Fare 45¢ each direction from either city.

Get up a party - reserve a coach and charter a 50 passenger bus from Saint Paul or Minneapolis to the Stadium. Ask our Agent for details covering all-expense Baseball excursion for your club or organization.

1962 Minnesota Twins Home Schedule

APRIL
LOS ANGELES—13, 14, 15(S)
CHICAGO—17, 18, 19
MAY
BALTIMORE—1, 2, 3
DETROIT—4, 5, 6(S)
CLEVELAND—8(N), 9(N), 10
KANSAS CITY—11(N), 12, 13(S)
BOSTON—28(N), 29
NEW YORK—30*
JUNE
WASHINGTON—1(N), 2, 3(S)
KANSAS CITY—5(N), 6(N), 7
CHICAGO 8(N), 9, 10(2)(S)
LOS ANGELES—22(N), 23, 24(2)(S)
JULY
NEW YORK—6(N), 7, 8(S)
ALL STAR GAME IN D.C.—10

WASHINGTON—12(N), 13(N), 14
BOSTON—15(2)(S)
CLEVELAND—17(N), 18, 19
BALTIMORE—20(N), 21, 22(S)
DETROIT—23(N), 24(N), 25(N)
AUGUST
NEW YORK—13(N), 14(N), 15(N), 16
BOSTON—17(TN2), 18, 19(S), 20
WASHINGTON—21(N), 22(N), 23(N)
KANSAS CITY—24(N), 25, 26(S)
SEPTEMBER
LOS ANGELES—10(N), 11
CHICAGO—12(N), 13
CLEVELAND—14(N), 15, 16(S)
DETROIT—18, 19, 20
BALTIMORE—28, 29, 30(S)

(N)—night game
(TN2)—twi-night doubleheader
(2)—afternoon doubleheader
(S)—Sunday afternoon

*—one game afternoon, one game night, separate admissions

The Seaboard Air Line's New York – Florida train services operated to and from New York over the connecting railroads north of Richmond. It is June 1940, and the train is shown here at Raleigh, North Carolina. The train provided sleeping and coach accommodations as well as dining and lounge car services. The train operated both to and from Miami and St. Petersburg. The Seaboard's No 257, a 4-8-2 built by Baldwin in 1925, is providing the power for the mixture of heavyweight and streamlined passenger equipment. *Harold K. Vollrath Collection*

CHAPTER 5

RAIL TRAVEL TO FLORIDA

Train travel to Florida was once provided not only from the New York City area, but also from the Midwest. There were several railroads involved. From New York City, the Pennsylvania Railroad handled the trains to Washington. From there it was the Richmond, Fredericksburg and Potomac which connected with the Atlantic Coast Line and the Seaboard Air Line. These two railroads handled the trains to Florida and the Gulf Coast, while the Miami-bound trains were interchanged with the Florida East Coast at Jacksonville. In 1953, trains from New York included:

Via Atlantic Coast Line Railroad

The Miamian
The Everglades
East Coast Champion
West Coast Champion
Havana Special
Florida Special — Seasonal train

Via Seaboard Air Line

The Silver Star
The Sunland
The Silver Meteor
The Palmland

The Midwest – Florida service was provided between Chicago and Florida and Detroit and Florida. The Chicago trains were handled by the Pennsylvania Railroad, the Illinois Central and the Chicago and Eastern Illinois. The PRR and C&EI trains were handed over to the Louisville and Nashville Railroad at Louisville and Evansville respectively. Depending upon the route, the L&N connected with the Atlantic Coast Line or the Central of Georgia. Trains again were interchanged with the Florida East Coast en route to Miami, or stayed with the ACL to the Gulf Coast.

The Pennsy trains to Florida included the Southland and the Southwind.

The Chicago and Eastern Illinois train services included the Dixie Flyer. Other C&EI trains to the south included the Georgian and the Humming Bird.

The Illinois Central trains included the Seminole and the City of Miami. This set of trains operated via the IC to Birmingham for a connection with the Central of Georgia. The CofG handled the trains to Albany for the connection with the Atlantic Coast Line. The trains to Miami were interchanged with the Florida East Coast.

All of the trains from the Chicago area, as well as the Detroit connection over the B&O to and from Cincinnati, were equipped with both sleeping and coach accommodations plus food and beverage service. The fastest trains operated out of Chicago or Florida in the morning and arrived at the destinations the next evening.

A variety of Florida services continued operating on the east coast right up until Amtrak. Service has continued between New York and Florida. However, the services from the Midwest have been absent for many years. There is talk of resuming the service, but there is nothing definite at this writing in early 2008.

It is July 1940, and the Atlantic Coast Line's Havana Special operated between New York and Miami with a second morning arrival. Other trains were providing faster schedules, but the Havana Special provided convenient times for the folks in between the Northeast and the Sunshine State. The Havana Special offered both sleeping and coach services along with dining and lounge facilities. Train 75 is shown here at North Charleston, South Carolina. Note the extensive head-end consist of six cars. *Harold K. Vollrath Collection*

The Atlantic Coast Line's West Coast Champion is pausing at Tampa, Florida, toward the end (and the start of Spring) of the full "Winter Season Travel" in this March 7, 1955, portrait. The train provided a full range of sleeping-car accommodations as well as comfortable coach seating between New York and the "West Coast" of Florida. *William Raia*

The ACL Florida trains were powered by the Pennsylvania GG-1s between New York and Washington, D. C. This streamlined ACL train is rolling through North Philadelphia with a heavyweight baggage car on the head-end. (July 12, 1964, William Raia)

The Seaboard's Silver Meteor is operating over the Pennsy trackage at Harrison, New Jersey, in June 1968. The train has a mixture of equipment such as the Atlantic Coast Line's baggage-dormitory car on the head-end followed by a Pennsylvania sleeping car. The third car is a lounge car with picture windows while the fourth car is a dining car. *William Raia*

The Seaboard Air Line's Silver Meteor, train No. 58, has three E-7 units for power as it pauses at Jacksonville in March 1958. *William Raia*

The primary Pennsylvania train between Chicago and Florida was the South Wind. What is interesting about the Chicago – Florida services is that there were three routes. Each of the route was scheduled for every three days during the summer, while the winter season service expanded to trains either daily or every other day. This varied from year to year depending upon the railroad and other factors. The South Wind is rolling through the South Side of Chicago with a streamlined 4-6-2 for power. There are seven cars in the streamlined consist on this winter day in 1937. As years progressed, the consists of the trains were expanded. Unfortunately, there is no direct Chicago – Florida service as this is being written in 2008. *Photo by P. Erlenberger, William Raia Collection*

Moving 18 years later to March 1955, the South Wind is pausing at Louisville, Kentucky, on the Louisville and Nashville Railroad with Atlantic Coast Line motive power heading up the train. The South Wind operated over the Pennsylvania, the L&N, the ACL and also the Florida East Coast. *William Raia*

One of the first streamlined trains between Chicago and Florida was the Illinois Central's City of Miami. It is shown here rolling along at 80 miles per hour with the 7-car consist for the original streamlined train in the early 1940s. This is double-track territory near Tuscola, Illinois. The City of Miami operated over the IC from Chicago to Birmingham, then over the Central of Georgia to Albany, the Atlantic Coast Line to Jacksonville, and finally the Florida East Coast the final distance to Miami. The train operated with morning departures from both Chicago and Miami, with arrival the second evening. The City of Miami operated on an every other day schedule in both directions. *Harold K. Vollrath Collection*

The IC's City of Miami became a very popular train. This view shows No. 53 en route to Florida arriving at Homewood, Illinois, in the late 1960s. (The IC's electrified commuter service trackage is behind the passenger train.) The train provided sleeping car service between Chicago and Miami, and also to Tampa-Sarasota and St. Petersburg. Coach service included the above listing plus St. Louis to Miami. Dining car service was available to all destinations and an observation-club-lounge car was part of the Chicago – Miami service. *Patrick C. Dorin*

The City of Miami is departing Homewood, Illinois, as the northbound Panama Limited, train No. 6, arrives at Homewood. *Patrick C. Dorin*

Moving forward to March 23, 1971, the City of Miami is shown here departing Flossmoor, Illinois. The train on this early spring day has a consist of 12 cars with a heavy passenger load. The IC color scheme was interrupted by three stainless steel Seaboard Coast Line passenger cars. The City of Miami was a train service that could be put to good use as we move forward into the 21st Century. *Patrick C. Dorin*

The Illinois Central dome coach No. 2201 was originally a Missouri Pacific car and was retired in 1971 after operating on the City of Miami. Although the car was stainless steel with corrugated sides, the car was painted in the IC color scheme of orange and brown when purchased by the IC in 1967. *John H. Kuehl, Patrick C. Dorin Collection*

A look back at a steam-powered Florida train, the Seminole, as it roars through French Village, Illinois, with the Louisville and Nashville 4-8-2, No. 414, in February, 1952. The seven-car train included coaches, sleeping cars and a diner-lounge car. *Harold K. Vollrath Collection*

A train service that is often not thought of during discussions about the need for Florida service was the Kansas City – Florida train operations on the St. Louis – San Francisco Railroad, known as the Frisco. This view shows the Kansas City – Florida Special at Kansas City in July 1940. The train operated over the Frisco from KC to Birmingham, and then over the Southern to Jacksonville, and Florida East Coast beyond. The KC-Florida Special is shown here with the Frisco 4-8-2, No. 1522, at Kansas City, Missouri. *Harold K. Vollrath Collection*

The Kansas City – Florida Special provided sleeping car service to Miami, plus coach service between Kansas City and Jacksonville. Coach passengers could change trains for service to Miami in the early 1950s. Dining and lounge-car service was also available between Kansas City and Birmingham, and partially over the remaining routes to Florida. The train did indeed have some heavy traffic levels as shown with the 11-car train near Shrewsbury, Missouri, in July 1951. By 1962 things were different. The train was still in operation with its name, and provided sleeping car and coach service between Kansas City and Jacksonville. Passengers needed to change trains for Miami and Tampa-St. Petersburg-Sarasota. A dining and a lounge car were part of the consist between Springfield and Birmingham in 1962. *Harold K. Vollrath Collection*

CHICAGO—INDIANAPOLIS—FLORIDA

READ DOWN			READ UP	
The South Wind See Note 1	Miles	Table 4 For dates of operation see note below	The South Wind See Note 1	
90 15 12-5		◄═══----------Pennsylvania R. R.----------═══► ◄═══----Louisville & Nashville R. R.----═══► ◄═══----Atlantic Coast Line R. R.----═══►	93 16 6-11	

AM			**PM**	
8.30	0	Lv **Chicago** (Un. Sta.)___(PRR) (C.S.T.) Ar	6.35	
e 8.44	7	" Englewood_____		
11.47	117	" Logansport (Van Sta.) " (E.S.T.) "	5.05	
1.37	202	" **Indianapolis**_____ " "	3.25	
3.55	313	Ar **Louisville**_____ " " Lv	12.55	
4.05	313	Lv Louisville_____(L&N) (E.S.T.) Ar	12.40	
e 5.05	427	" Bowling Green_____ " (C.S.T.) Lv	n 9.32	
6.28	500	Ar Nashville_____ " "	8.10	
e 8.44	620	" Decatur_____ " "	n 5.20	
10.23	705	" **Birmingham**_____ " "	3.50	
12.30	803	" Montgomery_____ " Ar	1.45	
12.35	803	Lv Montgomery_____(ACL) " Ar	1.30	
5.55	1013	Ar Thomasville_____ (E.S.T.) Lv	10.09	
7.55	1115	" Waycross(Okla.Ave.) " "	8.00	
9.25	1193	" **Jacksonville**_____ " Lv	6.40	
10.30	1193	Lv Jacksonville_____(ACL) (E.S.T.) Ar	5.20	
12.21	1300	Ar DeLand_____ " Lv	3.00	
12.45	1317	" Sanford_____ " "	2.35	
1.10	1335	" Winter Park_____ " "	2.10	
1.30	1340	" Orlando_____ " "	1.55	
2.20	1378	" Haines City_____ " "	1.08	
r 2.28	1385	" Lake Alfred_____ " "	1.00	
3.00	1400	Ar Lakeland_____ " Lv	12.40	
5.00	1475	Ar Punta Gorda_____(ACL) (E.S.T.) Lv	10.20	
5.45	1503	" Fort Myers_____ " "	9.45	
6.50	1539	" Naples_____ " Lv	8.45	
3.50	1431	Ar **Tampa**_____(ACL) (E.S.T.) Lv	12.01	
4.15	1431	Lv Tampa_____ " Ar	11.35	
5.15	1472	Ar Bradenton_____ " "	10.21	
5.35	1484	Ar **Sarasota**_____ " Lv	10 05	
10.25	1193	Lv Jacksonville_____(ACL) (E.S.T.) Ar	5.25	
12.20	1278	Ar Gainesville_____ " Lv	3.22	
1.22	1319	" Ocala_____ " "	2.17	
2.22	1353	" Leesburg_____ " "	1.16	
r 4.12	1436	" Tarpon Springs_____ " "	r11.21	
r 4.29	1446	" Dunedin_____ " "	r11.06	
4.39	1449	" Clearwater_____ " "	10.57	
5.15	1467	Ar **St. Petersburg**_____ " Lv	10.30	
9.55	1193	Lv Jacksonville_____(ACL) (E.S.T.) Ar	6.05	
11.59	1317	" Sanford_____ " "	3.10	
12.40	1340	" Orlando_____ " "	2.25	
♦ 4.05	1492	" West Palm Beach____ (SAL) "	♦10.53	
♦ 4.18	1499	" Lake Worth_____ " "	♦10.43	
♦ 4.30	1510	" Delray Beach_____ " "	♦10.30	
s 4.45	1518	" Boca Raton_____ " "	s10.19	
♦ 4.65	1526	" Pompano Beach_____ " "	♦10.14	
♦ 5.13	1534	" Fort Lauderdale_____ " "	♦10.05	
♦ 5.26	1541	" Hollywood_____ " "	♦ 9.50	
♦ 6.15	1559	Ar **Miami**_____ " Lv	♦ 9.25	
b11.30		Lv Jacksonville_____(BUS) E.S.T. Ar	b 5.20	
b12.20		Ar St. Augustine_____ " Lv	b 4.31	
b 1.40		" Daytona Beach_____ " "	b 3.24	
b 2.20		" New Smyrna Beach__ " "	b 2.42	
b 3.00		" Titusville_____ " "	b 2.05	
b 3.30		" Cocoa-Rockledge____ " "	b 1.36	
b 4.02		" Melbourne_____ " "	b 1.06	
b 4.45		" Vero Beach_____ " "	b12.25	
b 5.05		" Fort Pierce_____ " "	b12.05	
b 6.03		Ar Stuart_____ " Lv	b11.05	
PM			**AM**	

(left side vertical text: Operates Every Other Day — Sleeping Cars and Reserved Seat Coaches)
(right side vertical text: Operates Every Other Day — Sleeping Cars and Reserved Seat Coaches)

Reference Marks for Table 4

♦   SAL station used until further notice.
b   Greyhound bus connection to and from Jacksonville until further notice. Rail tickets not honored. Transfer at Jacksonville between railroad and bus stations by taxi upon payment of fare.
c   Stops only to receive passengers.
e   Stops only to discharge revenue passengers from Indianapolis or to receive revenue passengers for points south of Montgomery, Ala.
f   Stops only on signal or notice to agent or conductor to receive or discharge revenue passengers.
n   Stops to discharge revenue passengers from points south of Montgomery, Ala. or to receive revenue passengers for Indianapolis and beyond.
r   Stops to receive or discharge revenue passengers to or from Jacksonville and beyond.
s   SAL Station Deerfield Beach.

C.S.T.—Central Standard Time.
E.S.T.—Eastern Standard Time.

DATES OF OPERATION

Note 1.—**The South Wind**—Runs from Chicago and Miami even dates during January and April; odd dates during February and March.

Florida Service—Table 4—Equipment

SOUTHWARD

P. R. R. No. 90. THE SOUTH WIND
(For Dates of operation see Note 1)

Lounge Car (Bar)........Chicago to Miami (6 Double Bedrooms).
Sleeping Cars...Chicago to Miami—**Vista-Dome** (4 Roomettes, 4 Duplex Rooms, 4 Double Bedrooms). (24 Dome lounge seats for Pullman passengers only).
Chicago to Miami—(10 Roomettes, 6 Double Bedrooms). (Two Cars).
Chicago to Miami (4 Double Bedrooms, 4 Compartments, 2 Drawing Rooms).
Chicago to Tampa-Sarasota (4 Sections, 4 Roomettes, 5 Double Bedrooms, 1 Compartment).
Chicago to St. Petersburg (4 Sections, 4 Roomettes, 5 Double Bedrooms, 1 Compartment).
Chicago to Jacksonville (10 Roomettes, 6 Double Bedrooms).
Dining Cars....Chicago to Miami.
Jacksonville to Tampa.
Tavern Lounge.Jacksonville to Tampa.
Cafe Lounge....Jacksonville to St. Petersburg
Reclining Seat Coaches (All Seats Reserved—Coach Attendant Service)
Chicago to Miami.
Chicago to St. Petersburg.
Chicago to Tampa—Sarasota.
Lakeland to Naples.
For Special Service Charge in Reserved Seat Coaches, see Page 3.
Coach Lounge (Bar)........Chicago to Miami.

NORTHWARD

P. R. R. No. 93. THE SOUTH WIND
(For Dates of operation see Note 1)

Lounge Car (Bar).......Miami to Chicago (6 Double Bedrooms).
Sleeping Cars...Miami to Chicago—**Vista-Dome** (4 Roomettes, 4 Duplex Rooms, 4 Double Bedrooms). (24 Dome lounge seats for Pullman passengers only).
Miami to Chicago—(10 Roomettes, 6 Double Bedrooms). (Two Cars).
Miami to Chicago (4 Double Bedrooms, 4 Compartments, 2 Drawing Rooms).
Sarasota-Tampa to Chicago (4 Sections, 4 Roomettes, 5 Double Bedrooms, 1 Compartment).
St. Petersburg to Chicago (4 Sections, 4 Roomettes, 5 Double Bedrooms, 1 Compartment).
Jacksonville to Chicago (10 Roomettes, 6 Double Bedrooms).
Dining Cars....Miami to Chicago.
Tampa to Jacksonville.
Tavern Lounge.Tampa to Jacksonville.
Cafe Lounge....St. Petersburg to Jacksonville.
Reclining Seat Coaches (All Seats Reserved—Coach Attendant Service)
Miami to Chicago.
St. Petersburg to Chicago.
Sarasota—Tampa to Chicago.
Naples to Chicago.
For Special Service Charge in Reserved Seat Coaches, see Page 3.
Coach Lounge (Bar)........Miami to Chicago.

THE SOUTHWIND DEPARTURE CALENDAR, 1967
FROM CHICAGO AND MIAMI
Departure Dates in Bold Face

JANUARY								FEBRUARY								MARCH						
S	M	T	W	T	F	S		S	M	T	W	T	F	S		S	M	T	W	T	F	S
1	**2**	3	**4**	5	**6**	7					**1**	2	**3**	4					**1**	2	**3**	4
8	9	**10**	11	**12**	13	**14**		**5**	6	**7**	8	**9**	10	**11**		**5**	6	**7**	8	**9**	10	**11**
15	**16**	17	**18**	19	**20**	21		12	**13**	14	**15**	16	**17**	18		12	**13**	14	**15**	16	**17**	18
22	23	**24**	25	**26**	27	**28**		**19**	20	**21**	22	**23**	24	**25**		**19**	20	**21**	22	**23**	24	**25**
29	**30**	**31**						26	**27**	28						**26**	27	**28**	29	**30**	**31**	

APRIL								MAY								JUNE						
S	M	T	W	T	F	S		S	M	T	W	T	F	S		S	M	T	W	T	F	S
						1			1	2	3	4	5	6						1	2	3
2	3	**4**	5	**6**	7	**8**		7	**8**	9	**10**	11	**12**	13		4	**5**	6	**7**	8	**9**	10
9	**10**	11	**12**	13	**14**	15		**14**	15	**16**	17	**18**	19	**20**		**11**	12	**13**	14	**15**	16	**17**
16	**17**	18	**19**	20	**21**	22		21	**22**	23	**24**	25	**26**	27		18	**19**	20	**21**	22	**23**	24
23	**24**	25	**26**	27	**28**	29		**28**	29	**30**	31					**25**	26	**27**	28	**29**	**30**	
30																						

LIBERAL BAGGAGE PRIVILEGES, TOO! Take the "Lug" out of Luggage—See pages 4 & 5.

The South Wind operated over the Pennsylvania, the Louisville and Nashville, the Atlantic Coast Line and the Seaboard Air Line between Chicago and Miami. Table No. 4 from the January 26, 1967, PRR timetables illustrates the type of equipment and the train schedule for the 1559 mile route.

It is August 1965, and the Santa Fe's Fort Worth section of the Texas Chief is shown here at Gainesville, Texas. The consist of 17 cars includes chair cars, food and beverage equipment, sleeping cars and four head-end cars, one of which is a 60-foot Rail Post Office car. Also, the stop at Gainesville was where the Dallas and Fort Worth sections were either split or combined depending upon the direction to and from Chicago. *Lloyd Keyser*

CHAPTER 6

THE MIDWEST TO THE GULF COAST and TEXAS

There were some rather interesting long distance train services between Chicago, St. Louis, and Cincinnati and the Lone Star State of Texas and the Gulf Coast. Railroads such as the Louisville and Nashville, Chicago and Eastern Illinois, the Missouri Pacific, the Frisco, the Texas and Pacific, and the Missouri-Kansas-Texas provided a wide variety of train services and frequencies.

The routes south of Chicago to the Gulf Coast included the Illinois Central as a direct operation, with the C&EI providing interchange operations with the L&N and the Nashville, Chattanooga, and St. Louis lines for through service to areas such as Atlanta, New Orleans and many stations in between. Trains

included such operations as the Panama Limited, the City of New Orleans, the Humming Bird, the Pan American and more.

The long distance services between Chicago and St. Louis and the Lone Star State of Texas were via the Gulf, Mobile and Ohio and Missouri Pacific, and the Santa Fe. There was also a Rock Island train service between the Twin Cities and Texas. So at one time folks had a number of trains to choose from for traveling to and from Texas or the Midwest.

The long distance trains included Texas Eagles on the Missouri Pacific and the Texas Chief on the Santa Fe along with additional secondary trains. The Rock Island named their train the Twin Star

Rocket, which was appropriate for operating between the North Star State of Minnesota and the Lone Star State of Texas.

St. Louis and Texas services were also provided by the Frisco and the Missouri-Kansas & Texas Railroads with a train known as the Texas Special. The MKT, known as the Katy, also operated through trains between Kansas City and Texas. The Rock Island operated the Texas Rocket between Kansas City and Fort Worth.

There was also a joint train operated by the Burlington and the Rock Island providing service between Minneapolis and St. Louis. It was known as the Zephyr Rocket. All of the trains mentioned above provided both sleeping and coach accommodations as well as food and beverage service.

The 1950s was a great time for such travel between the Midwest and Texas, but the service rapidly evaporated moving toward the 1960s and by the time of Amtrak, it was gone. The following photos and timetables illustrate the many types of train operations between the Upper Midwest and the South.

This photo illustrates the five-car consist of the Dallas section at Gainesville. *Lloyd Keyser*

The five cars of the Dallas section are shown here being added to the Fort Worth section for a grand total of 22 cars. There is no doubt about it, the Texas Chief was one of the finest trains to be operated between Chicago and Texas. *Lloyd Keyser*

The City of New Orleans was the all-coach daytime run between Chicago and New Orleans. The train included dining car service as well as a St. Louis section between St. Louis and Carbondale, Illinois. The final car of the train was a tavern-lounge observation car. This photo shows train No. 1 with seven cars in the late 1960s just south of Chicago at Homewood. No. 1 departed Chicago at 7:50 a.m. and arrived in New Orleans at 12:25 a.m. for the 921.1-mile route. Northbound No. 2 departed New Orleans at 7:15 a.m. and arrived in Chicago at 11:40 p.m. during the late 1950s. *Patrick C. Dorin*

It is May 1948, and a train known as the Orelanean is at DeQuincy, Louisiana, on the Missouri Pacific's subsidiary, the New Orleans, Texas & Mexico. This particular train provided day train service between New Orleans and Houston, 367.4 miles. The consist of the train included coaches and an observation-parlor-dining car. The time schedule during the 1940s was in the area of 10 hours, 30 minutes for both directions. What is interesting is that this particular train also carried a through sleeping car between New Orleans and Oakland. *Harold K. Vollrath Collection*

The Katy Flyer on the Missouri-Kansas & Texas Railroad was a St. Louis and Kansas City train to San Antonio. A section of the train operated to and from St. Louis over the Frisco. The train included both Dallas and Fort Worth sections and provided sleeping and coach services. This portrait of the Katy Flyer is train No. 26, which was the Kansas City section. *Harold K. Vollrath Collection*

This Missouri Pacific train was known as the Sunshine Special, which had numerous origins and destinations. Basically a St. Louis – Shreveport, Louisiana train, the service included routes to El Dorado, Lake Charles and Hot Springs. There were sleeping car services plus a diner-lounge and coaches as part of the various consists. This section of the train is shown here at Alexandria, Louisiana, in April 1948, and has but five cars including two head-end cars, two coaches and one sleeping car. *Harold K. Vollrath Collection*

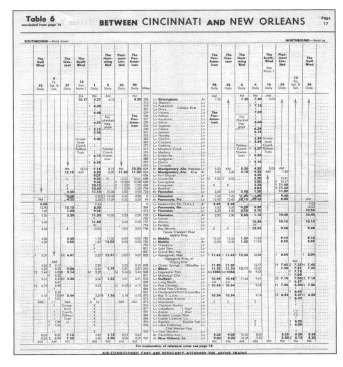

The L&N Time Table No. 6 (Spring, 1958) illustrates the service levels between Cincinnati and the Gulf Coast and New Orleans.

The history of convenient transcontinental train services goes back to the 1920s (and even before that) and led to the introduction in the 1930s of faster schedules, streamliners and eventually to domeliners and hi-level cars. This photo shows the Texas and New Orleans and Southern Pacific's train No. 1, the Sunset Limited, rolling through New Iberia, Louisiana, in May 1939. The train consists of eleven cars including three head-end cars plus coaches, sleeping cars and food and beverage cars. It was the best way to travel between New Orleans and Los Angeles. *Harold K. Vollrath Collection*

CHAPTER 7

TRANSCONTINENTAL TRAIN SERVICES

The ultimate in long distance rail travel was (and is) the transcontinental train services. North America during the middle of the 20th Century had several transcontinental routes extending from eastern Canada to Vancouver, Chicago to California, Oregon and Washington, St. Louis to the West Coast, and finally from New Orleans to Los Angeles. The service included fast streamliner service with some schedules taking less than 40 hours between Chicago and California, plus numerous secondary trains and mail trains. A brief review of the trains in operation included the following on page 75.

All of the trains provided both sleeping and coach accommodations with the exception of the Great Northern's Fast Mail. This particular train had one or two coaches plus a baggage car as the rear car equipped with flagman's compartment.

The following photos and timetables illustrate the types of train services for various periods of time during the 1950s and '60s.

Railroad	Trains	Notes
Canadian Pacific	Canadian Dominion	Montreal – Toronto Vancouver
Canadian National	Super Continental Continental	Montreal – Toronto Vancouver
Soo Line	The Soo-Dominion Mountaineer	Minneapolis St Paul– Vancouver
Great Northern with Burlington	Empire Builder Western Star Fast Mail	Chicago and Twin Cities Seattle and Portland
Northern Pacific	North Coast Limited Mainstreeter	Chicago and Twin Cities Seattle and Portland
Milwaukee Road	Olympian Hiawatha Columbian	Chicago – Seattle – Tacoma
Union Pacific with C&NW	City of San Francisco City of Portland City of Los Angeles Los Angeles Limited San Francisco Overland Portland Rose Note: Southern Pacific participated with the City of San Francisco and the Overland	Chicago – San Francisco Chicago – Portland Chicago – Los Angeles Chicago – Los Angeles Chicago – San Francisco Chicago – Portland
Burlington with Rio Grande and Western Pacific	California Zephyr	Chicago – San Francisco
Union Pacific with the Wabash	City of St. Louis	St. Louis – Los Angeles
Santa Fe	Super Chief El Capitan The Chief Grand Canyon San Francisco Chief California Limited	Chicago – Los Angeles Chicago – San Francisco
Southern Pacific	Sunset Limited Argonaut	New Orleans – Los Angeles
Rock Island with Southern Pacific	Golden State Imperial	Chicago – Los Angeles

During the days of steam, the length of transcontinentals often required double headers. This is the case with two streamlined 2-10-4s heading up the Canadian Pacific's Dominion through the Rockies in June 1948. During that period of time, the Dominion not only served the Montreal – Toronto – Vancouver route, but also was combined with a train between Calgary and Vancouver from the Soo Line, known as the Soo-Dominion. The train had a mixed consist of both Soo Line and Canadian Pacific passenger equipment. During the summer season, the Soo-Dominion was replaced by a separate train, the Mountaineer, between St. Paul and Vancouver. *Harold K. Vollrath Collection*

Since 1929, the Great Northern operated two well-patronized transcontinental trains, the Empire Builder and the Oriental Limited. This view shows the Oriental Limited, train No. 4, in April 1947 at Minot, North Dakota. The two sets of trains were scheduled about 10 to 12 hours apart, which provided convenient schedules for the cities and towns along the route between Chicago and Seattle-Portland. *Harold K. Vollrath Collection*

The Great Northern's Empire Builder is racing through Savanna, Illinois, over the Burlington Route trackage. The GN transcontinental service was also handled by the Burlington between Chicago and St. Paul and the Spokane, Portland and Seattle between Spokane and Portland. The Portland and Seattle sections of the Builder were split or combined at Spokane. *Frank Schnick*

Frank Schnick photographed the North Coast Limited at Savanna on the same day in 1966 as the Empire Builder, illustrated in this section. The North Coast Limited provided the same types of services as the Builder, which included sleeping car accommodations, chair cars with leg-rest seating for the ultimate comfort, plus the dining and lounge facilities. The North Coast Limited also included a slumber-coach, which was a high capacity sleeping car that provided accommodations with a coach level fare, plus the type of sleeper room fare. *Frank Schnick*

Burlington Route power generally handled the NP and GN trains between St. Paul and Chicago. In order to trade motive power hours, the Burlington also used GN power on its freight trains. This photo shows two Burlington E units heading up the eastbound Empire Builder during the summer of 1966. *Frank Schnick*

It is March 1949, and the new Domeliner California Zephyr is on a display trip at Galesburg, Illinois. The train went into service on March 20th of that year. The display train was powered by one E-5 diesel, the 9915, and consisted of eight cars including the dome coaches, a dome lounge car, a dining car, sleeping cars and the dome observation lounge sleeping car. The California Zephyr operated over the Burlington between Chicago and Denver; the Denver, Rio Grande and Western between Denver and Salt Lake City; and the Western Pacific between Salt Lake and Oakland-San Francisco. The train ran over the Rio Grande through the Rockies during the daylight hours providing travelers with new levels of knowledge about the Rocky Mountains. *Harold K. Vollrath Collection*

The Northern Pacific eventually equipped the North Coast Limited with both dome sleepers and dome coaches. The train is shown here during a station stop at Butte, Montana. The train to the left is quite likely a passenger extra pausing at the Butte station, since 25 was scheduled for about 3:45 p.m., while eastbound 26 stopped at Butte at 7:40 a.m. *Harold K. Vollrath Collection*

Seattle was the western destination for both the North Coast Limited and the Great Northern's Empire Builder. The Seattle section of the North Coast is at Seattle with its nine-car consist. The North Coast Limited's Portland and Seattle sections were split at Pasco, Washington, with the Portland section operating over the Spokane, Portland Seattle Railway. The eastbound trains to Chicago were combined at Pasco. Although a bit difficult to see in the background of the photo, the Seattle section has but one dome coach and one dome sleeping car, since the other two dome cars operated on the train to Portland. *William Raia.*

This is a rather interesting photo of a Milwaukee Road electric No. E-4 on what appears to be either a passenger extra or a second section of the Olympian Hiawatha. The train is in electrified territory on the Milwaukee Road at Missoula, Montana. The first car on the train is actually a Pennsylvania Railroad observation car, but it is not possible to see the name or identify the type of car. The Milwaukee Road's Olympian Hiawatha was one of the primary trains operated by the three railroads operating between the Midwest and Seattle. *Harold K. Vollrath Collection*

It is May 1963, and train No. 10, the Union Pacific's City of St. Louis, is departing Los Angeles and heading eastward toward St. Louis, Missouri. The ten cars (including three head-end cars) are providing leg-rest chair car seating and a wide variety of sleeping car accommodations. The dining and lounge cars will provide the passengers ample time for meals and new levels of comfort to meet new friends. And incidentally, many marriages came together because folks met each other on the train, and had a chance to get to know one another before dating began. *Thomas Dorin Collection*

The Union Pacific operated a coordinated transcontinental service with the Wabash, Chicago and North Western (later the Milwaukee Road) and the Southern Pacific for its fleet of transcontinental trains. This view shows the eastbound City of St. Louis at Laramie, Wyoming, en route from Los Angeles to St. Louis on June 2, 1963. Four E units were needed to power the long trains, which were popular with the traveling public. *Herman Page*

Motive power from the various railroads handled the UP transcontinentals. In this May 21, 1963, scene, two Wabash E units are heading up the City of St. Louis near Kansas City. The eleven-car Domeliner also includes four head-end cars with a box express car and an RPO-baggage. *Herman Page*

The Santa Fe's westbound Chief departed Chicago in the morning and arrived in Los Angeles the next evening. Passengers spent two days on the train with one night en route. It provided an opportunity to see more of the scenery between Chicago and LA. The eastbound Chief departed LA around 12:00 noon and arrived at Chicago around 7:15 a.m. the second morning. Not only did the train provide an early arrival in Chicago from LA, but also provided overnight service from Kansas City to Chicago. The train was equipped with a Big Dome as part of the food and beverage service equipment. Unfortunately, the Chief was discontinued in 1968. *Herman Page*

The Union Pacific's combined City of Los Angeles and City of San Francisco, train No. 104, is shown here operating on a detour over the Rock Island Railroad through Iowa due to a derailment on the Milwaukee Road. The combined train had a consist of over twenty cars and required four units even through the prairies to and from Chicago. The date is May 1, 1965. *William S. Kuba*

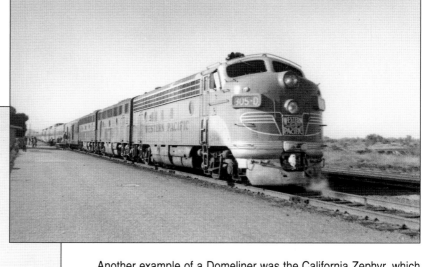

Another example of a Domeliner was the California Zephyr, which operated over the Burlington, the Denver, Rio Grande and Western, and the Western Pacific between Chicago and Oakland, California. This view shows the train on the WP. The consist included three dome coaches, a dome buffet-lounge and finally a dome observation-sleeper. The train traveled through the Rockies during the daytime hours on the Rio Grande Railroad providing an opportunity to see the beautiful scenery. The train also traveled through the Moffet Tunnel, which was over six miles long. *William S. Kuba*

Still another Domeliner to the north in Canada was the Canadian Pacific's Canadian, which operated between Montreal, Toronto and Vancouver. This view was taken in June 1969 as Jim Scribbins was aboard train No. 2 between Winnipeg and Thunder Bay. The three head-end cars had the Canadian Pacific maroon letterboard, while the diesel power and the passenger cars were in the CP Rail image. The consist of the train on this trip included two dining cars as well as a dome buffet-lounge and the dome observation sleeper with a total number of 18 cars. *Jim Scribbins*

This photo from May 1957 illustrates the Toronto section of the Canadian, train No. 11, alongside the afternoon departure of an RDC train bound for Windsor and Detroit. Train 11 is about to depart for Sudbury, Ontario, to connect and combine with train No. 1 from Montreal to Vancouver. Trains 11 and 12 were examples of how trains could be coordinated to serve the transcontinental route between Montreal, Toronto and the Pacific Coast. *Jim Scribbins*

The dome observation-sleeper, the Banff Park brings up the rear of train CP No. 1 with a 13-car consist at Ignace, Ontario, in September 1971. *Jim Scribbins*

The combined City streamliner, sometimes called the "City of Everywhere" is running westbound as train No. 103 at Savanna, Illinois, on the Milwaukee Road in September 1969. The motive power includes a Milwaukee Road FP-7 and an F45. *Lloyd Keyser*

The Cab-Forward Steam Power of the Southern Pacific provided ample power for such trains as the San Francisco Overland. No. 27 has 16 cars on this bright June 1950 day out west. *W. C. Whittaker*

Many of the transcontinental trains carried passenger equipment with the train name on the side of the equipment. Two examples of heavy-weight coaches for the UP's Challenger between Chicago and California were the 1220 and 504. Note the position of the words, "The Challenger" on the car center. The cars were photographed at East Los Angeles in February 1947. *William C. Whittaker*

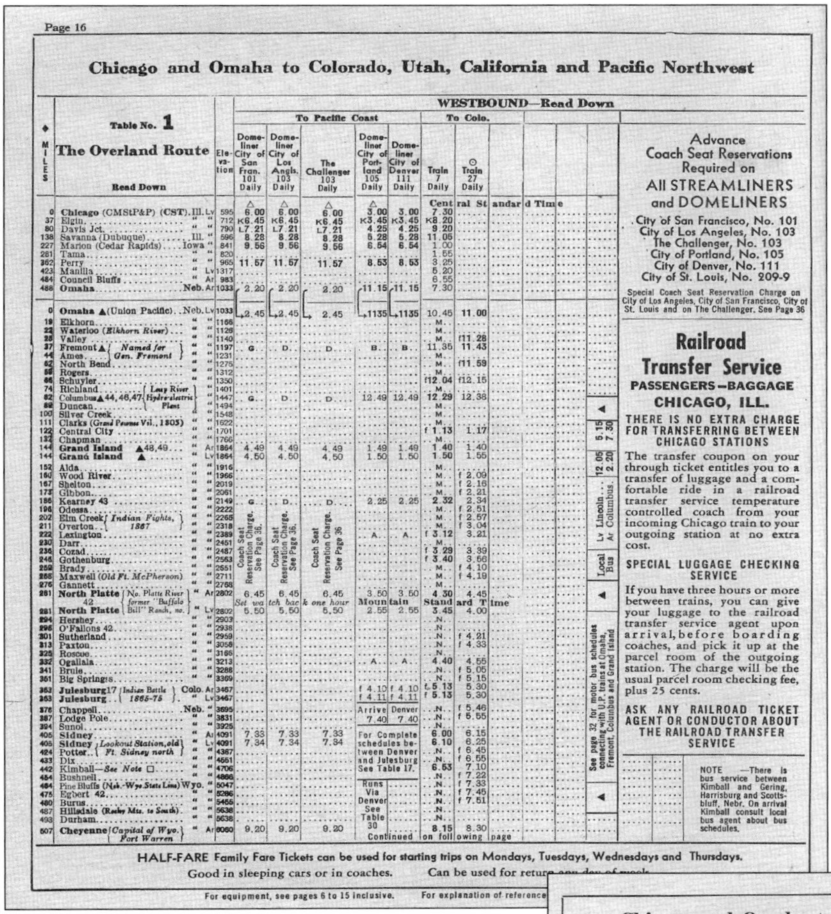

The westbound schedules from the Union Pacific April 1964 illustrate the fleet of passenger trains between Chicago and the West Coast operated by the UP, the Milwaukee Road and Southern Pacific.

Page 16 (left table)

Chicago and Omaha to Colorado, Utah, California and Pacific Northwest

Table No. 1 — The Overland Route

WESTBOUND—Read Down

MILES	Read Down	Elevation	Domeliner City of San Fran. 101 Daily	Domeliner City of Los Angls. 103 Daily	The Challenger 103 Daily	Domeliner City of Portland 105 Daily	Domeliner City of Denver 111 Daily	Train 1 Daily	Train 27 Daily	Advance Coach Seat Reservations
			To Pacific Coast			To Colo.				
								Central Standard Time		
0	Chicago (CMStP&P) (CST.) Ill. Lv	595	6.00	6.00	6.00	3.00	3.00	7.30		Required on ALL STREAMLINERS and DOMELINERS
37	Elgin, "	712	K6.45	K6.45	K6.45	K3.45	K3.45	K8.20		City of San Francisco, No. 101
80	Davis Jct. "	790	L7.21	L7.21	L7.21	4.25	4.25	9.20		City of Los Angeles, No. 103
138	Savanna (Dubuque) Ill. "	596	8.28	8.28	8.28	5.28	5.28	11.06		The Challenger, No. 103
227	Marion (Cedar Rapids) Iowa "	841	9.56	9.56	9.56	6.54	6.54	1.00		City of Portland, No. 105
281	Tama, "	830						1.55		City of Denver, No. 111
362	Perry, "	965	11.57	11.57	11.57	8.63	8.63	3.25		City of St. Louis, No. 209-9
423	Manilla " Lv	1317						5.20		
484	Council Bluffs " Ar	983						6.55		Special Coach Seat Reservation Charge on City of Los Angeles, City of San Francisco, City of St. Louis and on The Challenger. See Page 36
488	Omaha Neb. Ar	1033	2.20	2.20	2.20	11.15	11.15	7.30		
0	Omaha (Union Pacific) Neb. Lv	1033	2.45	2.45	2.45	1135	1135	10.45	11.00	**Railroad Transfer Service** PASSENGERS—BAGGAGE CHICAGO, ILL.
19	Elkhorn, "	1166						M...		THERE IS NO EXTRA CHARGE FOR TRANSFERRING BETWEEN CHICAGO STATIONS
29	Waterloo (Elkhorn River) "	1185						M...		The transfer coupon on your through ticket entitles you to a transfer of luggage and a comfortable ride in a railroad transfer service temperature controlled coach from your incoming Chicago train to your outgoing station at no extra cost.
33	Valley "	1140						M...	f11.28	
46	Fremont Named for Gen. Fremont "	1197	G...		B...	B...	11.35	11.43		
51	Ames "	1231						M...	f11.59	
60	North Bend "	1275						M...		
68	Rogers, "	1304						M...		
86	Schuyler, "	1330						M...	f12.04 f12.15	
74	Richland, Loup River "	1401				12.49	12.49	12.29 12.38		
80	Columbus 44,46,47, Hydro-electric Plant "	1442	G...	D...	D...			M...		
99	Duncan "	1494						M...	7.30	SPECIAL LUGGAGE CHECKING SERVICE
110	Silver Creek "	1548						M...		If you have three hours or more between trains, you can give your luggage to the railroad transfer service agent upon arrival, before boarding coaches, and pick it up at the parcel room of the outgoing station. The charge will be the usual parcel room checking fee, plus 25 cents.
111	Clarks (Grand Prairie Vil., 1805) "	1602						M...	1.17	
122	Central City "	1701						M...	1.13	
132	Chapman "	1766						M...		
144	Grand Island 48,49... Ar	1864	4.49	4.49	4.49	1.49	1.49	1.40	1.40	
144	Grand Island Lv	1864	4.50	4.50	4.50	1.50	1.50	1.50	1.55	
152	Alda, "	1916						M...		
160	Wood River "	1966						M...	f 2.09	
170	Shelton, "	2019						M...	f 2.16	
173	Gibbon, "	2061						M...	f 2.21	
184	Kearney 43 "	2149	G...	D...	D...			M...	f 2.34	
196	Odessa, "	2222				2.25	2.25	2.32	2.51	ASK ANY RAILROAD TICKET AGENT OR CONDUCTOR ABOUT THE RAILROAD TRANSFER SERVICE
202	Elm Creek Indian Fights, 1867 "	2265						M...	f 2.57	
211	Overton "	2318						M...	f 3.04	
222	Lexington "	2389						A...	3.12	3.21
231	Darr, "	2451						M...		
236	Cozad, "	2487						M...	f 3.29	3.39
245	Gothenburg, "	2552						M...	f 3.40	3.66
255	Brady, "	2651						M...	f 4.10	
266	Maxwell (Old Ft. McPherson) "	2711						M...	f 4.16	
272	Gannett... "	2766						M...		
281	North Platte No. Platte River 42 former Buffalo Bill's Ranch, no. Ar	2802	6.45	6.45	6.45	3.50	3.50	4.30	4.45	
281	North Platte " Lv	2802	5.50	5.50	5.50	2.55	2.55	3.45	4.00	
294	Hershey "	2909						N...		
300	O'Fallons 42 "	2938						N...	f 4.21	
301	Sutherland "	2959						N...		
313	Paxton, "	3058						N...	f 4.33	
332	Roscoe, "	3166						N...		
332	Ogalalla "	3213						N...	f 4.40	4.55
341	Brule, "	3288						N...	f 5.05	
361	Big Springs "	3369						N...		
363	Julesburg Indian Battle Colo. Ar	3457				f 4.10 f 4.10		5.13	5.30	
363	Julesburg 1865-75 Lv	3467				4.11 f 4.11		5.13	5.30	
383	Chappell, Neb. "	3695				Arrive Denver 7.40		N...	5.46	
387	Lodge Pole, "	3831				7.40		N...	5.55	
394	Sunol, "	3925						N...		
405	Sidney Lookout Station,old "	4091	7.33	7.33	7.33	For Complete schedules between Denver and Julesburg See Table 17		6.00	6.15	
405	Sidney Ft. Sidney north "	4091	7.34	7.34	7.34			6.10	6.25	
423	Potter, "	4387						N...	f 6.45	
423	Dix "	4461						N...	f 6.65	
442	Kimball—See Note "	4706						N...	6.53	7.10
454	Bushnell, "	4865						N...	f 7.20	
464	Pine Bluffs (Nbr.-Wyo.State Line) Wyo. "	5047				Runs via Denver See Table 30		N...	f 7.33	
476	Egbert 42 "	5296						N...	f 7.45	
480	Burns, "	5456						N...	7.50	
487	Hillsdale (Rocky Mts. to South) "	5638						N...	f 8.00	
493	Durham, "	5636						N...		
507	Cheyenne Capital of Wyo. Fort Warren Ar	6060	9.20	9.20	9.20	8.15	8.15	8.30		
						Continued on following page				

HALF-FARE Family Fare Tickets can be used for starting trips on Mondays, Tuesdays, Wednesdays and Thursdays.
Good in sleeping cars or in coaches. Can be used for return any day of week.

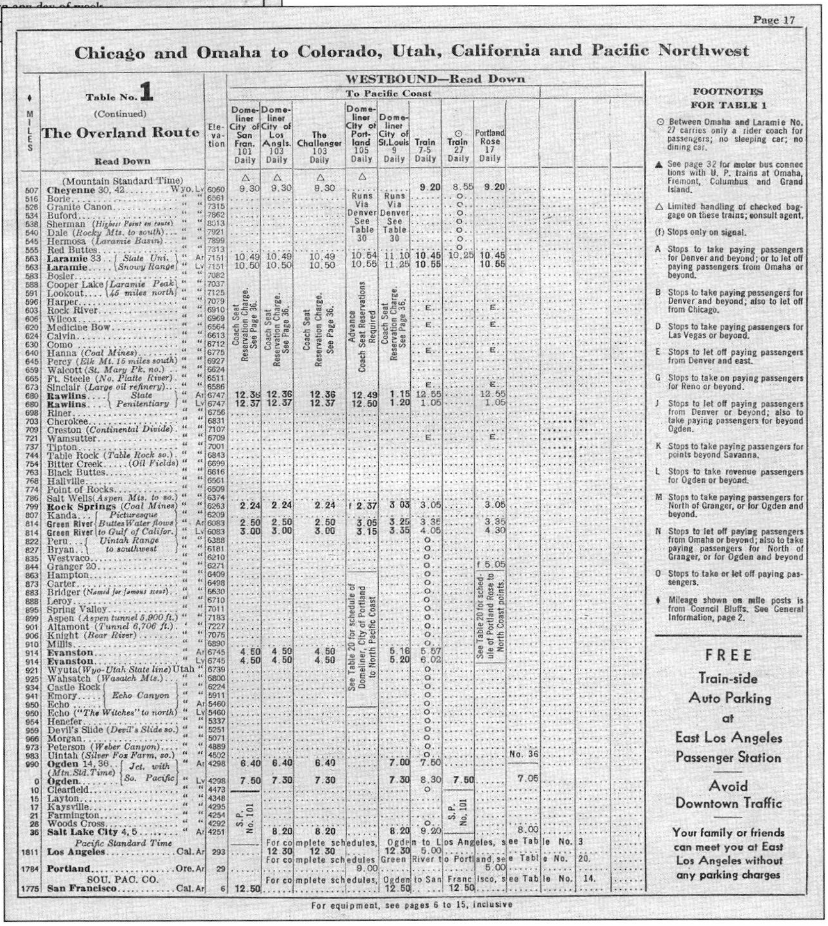

For equipment, see pages 6 to 15 inclusive. For explanation of reference...

Margin notes (right side): Central Standard Time / 5.15 / 12.05 / 2.20 / Lv Lincoln Ar Columbus / Local Bus / See page 32 for motor bus schedules connecting with U.P. trains at Omaha, Fremont, Columbus and Grand Island. / NOTE —There is bus service between Kimball and Gering, Harrisburg and Scottsbluff, Nebr. On arrival Kimball consult local bus agent about bus schedules.

Page 17 (right table)

Chicago and Omaha to Colorado, Utah, California and Pacific Northwest

Table No. 1 (Continued) — The Overland Route

WESTBOUND—Read Down

MILES	Read Down	Elevation	Domeliner City of San Fran. 101 Daily	Domeliner City of Los Angls. 103 Daily	The Challenger 103 Daily	Domeliner City of Portland 105 Daily	Domeliner City of St.Louis 9 Daily	Train 1 Daily	Train 27 Daily	Portland Rose Daily
			To Pacific Coast							
			(Mountain Standard Time)							
507	Cheyenne 30, 42 Wyo. Lv	6060	9.30	9.30	9.30			9.20	8.55	9.20
516	Borie, "	6561				Runs via Denver See Table 30	Runs via Denver See Table 30	O...	O...	
524	Huford "	7315						O...		
534	Buford "	7852						O...		
540	Sherman (Highest Point en route) "	8013						O...		
540	Dale (Rocky Mts. to south) "	7991						O...		
546	Hermosa (Laramie Basin) "	7899						O...		
555	Red Dalton "	7353						O...		
563	Laramie 33 State Uni. Ar	7151	10.49	10.49	10.49	10.54	11.10	10.45	10.25	10.45
563	Laramie Snowy Range Lv	7151	10.50	10.50	10.50	10.58	11.25	10.55		10.55
573	Bosler "	7082						O...		
588	Cooper Lake Laramie Peak "	7037						O...		
591	Lookout 46 miles north "	7125						O...		
596	Harper, "	7079						O...		
603	Rock River "	6910						E...		
610	Wilcox "	6969						O...		
620	Medicine Bow "	6564						O...		
626	Calvin, "	6712						O...		
630	Como "	6712						E...		
640	Hanna (Coal Mines) "	6775						O...		
645	Percy (Elk Mt.15 miles south) "	6824						O...		
649	Walcott (St. Mary Pk.no.) "	6624						O...		
655	Ft. Steele (No. Platte River) "	6511						E...		
665	Sinclair (Large oil refinery). "	6586						O...		
680	Rawlins State Ar	6747	12.3s	12.36	12.36	12.49	1.15	12.55		12.55
680	Rawlins Penitentiary Lv	6747	12.37	12.37	12.37	12.50	1.20	1.05		1.05
698	Riner "	6756						O...		
703	Cherokee "	6831						E...		
709	Creston (Continental Divide) "	7107						O...		
721	Wamsutter "	6709						O...		
721	Tipton "	6843						O...		
744	Table Rock (Table Rock so.) "	6843						E...		
754	Bitter Creek (Oil Fields) "	6699						O...		
763	Black Buttes "	6591						O...		
768	Hallville, "	6509						O...		
774	Point of Rocks "	6457						E...		
786	Salt Wells (Aspen Mts. to so.) "	6354						O...		
799	Rock Springs (Coal Mines) "	6263	2.24	2.24	2.24	2.37	3.03	3.05		3.05
805	Kanda Picturesque "	6209						O...		
814	Green River Buttes/Water Rocks "	6063	2.50	2.50	2.50	3.05	3.35	3.35		3.35
814	Green River to Gulf of Califor. "	6083	3.00	3.00	3.00	3.15	3.55	4.05		4.30
823	Peru Uintah Range to southwest "	6288						O...		
827	Bryan "	6181						O...		
835	Westvaco, "	6271						O...		
844	Granger 20 "	6409						5.05		
863	Hampton, "	6498						O...		
873	Carter, "	6710						O...		
883	Bridger (Named for famous scout) "	6630						O...		
890	Leroy "	7011						O...		
895	Spring Valley "	7183						O...		
899	Aspen (Aspen tunnel 3,900 ft.) "	7227						O...		
901	Altamont (Tunnel 6,706 ft.) "	7075				See Table 20 for schedule of Domeliner, City of Portland to North Pacific Coast	See Table 20 for sched-ule of Portland Rose to North Coast points	O...		
906	Knight (Bear River) "	6930						O...		
911	Mills... "	6745						O...		
914	Evanston Ar	6745	4.50	4.50	4.50	5.16	5.57			
914	Evanston Lv	6745	4.50	4.50	4.50	5.20	6.02			
925	Wyuta (Wyo.-Utah State line) Utah "	6800						O...		
925	Wahsatch (Wasatch Mts.) "	6800						O...		
934	Castle Rock "	6911						O...		
941	Emory Echo Canyon "	5460						O...		
950	Echo "	5460						O...		
955	Echo ("The Witches" to north) "	5337						O...		
954	Henefer "	5251						O...		
959	Devil's Slide (Devil's Slide no.) "	5251						O...		
966	Morgan, "	4889						O...		
973	Peterson (Weber Canyon), "	4602						O...		
980	Uintah (Silver Fox Farm, so.) "	4502						O...		
989	Ogden 14,36, Jct. with (Mtn.Std.Time) " Ar	4298	6.40	6.40	6.49	7.00	7.50		No. 36	
0	Ogden So. Pacific Lv	4298	7.50	7.30	7.30	7.30	8.30	7.50		7.05
10	Clearfield "	4473						O...		
14	Layton, "	4348						O...		
19	Kaysville "	4295						O...		
21	Farmington, "	4294						O...		
25	Woods Cross "	4292						O...		
36	Salt Lake City 4,5 Ar	4297	S.P. No. 101 8.20	8.20	8.20	8.20	9.20	S.P. No. 101 9.20		8.00
	Pacific Standard Time									
1811	Los Angeles Cal. Ar	293	For complete schedules 12.30	12.30	12.30	For complete schedules, Ogden to Los Angeles, see Table No. 3				
1784	Portland Ore. Ar	29			9.00		5.00	Green River to Portland (p.m.) see Table No. 20.		
1775	San Francisco SOU. PAC. CO. Cal. Ar	6	12.50	For complete schedules Green River to San Franc isco, see Table No. 14.	12.50		12.50			

For equipment, see pages 6 to 15, inclusive.

FOOTNOTES FOR TABLE 1

⊙ Between Omaha and Laramie No. 27 carries only a rider coach for passengers; no sleeping car; no dining car.

▲ See page 32 for motor bus connections with U. P. trains at Omaha, Fremont, Columbus and Grand Island.

△ Limited number of checked baggage on these trains; consult agent.

(f) Stops only on signal.

A Stops to take paying passengers for Denver and beyond; or to let off paying passengers from Omaha or beyond.

B Stops to take paying passengers for Denver and beyond; also to let off from Chicago.

D Stops to take paying passengers for Las Vegas or beyond.

E Stops to let off paying passengers from Denver and east.

G Stops to take paying passengers for Reno or beyond.

J Stops to let off paying passengers from Denver or beyond; also to take paying passengers for beyond Ogden.

K Stops to take paying passengers for points beyond Savanna.

L Stops to take revenue passengers for Ogden or beyond.

M Stops to take paying passengers for North of Granger, or for Ogden and beyond.

N Stops to let off paying passengers from Omaha or beyond; also to take paying passengers for North of Granger, or for Ogden and beyond

O Stops to take or let off paying passengers.

♦ Mileage shown on mile posts is from Council Bluffs. See General Information, page 2.

FREE Train-side Auto Parking at East Los Angeles Passenger Station

Avoid Downtown Traffic

Your family or friends can meet you at East Los Angeles without any parking charges.

It is May 1948, and mail services with the Rail Post Offices as part of the baggage-car design were a high priority. This photo illustrates a Chicago, St. Paul, Minneapolis and Omaha Railway train loading mail in the RPO to the right at Omaha, Nebraska. The Omaha, as the CStPM&O was known, operated trains between Omaha and St. Paul-Minneapolis. RPO services were provided throughout the entire US and Canada. *Harold K. Vollrath Collection*

CHAPTER 8

MAIL and EXPRESS TRAIN and SERVICE

The North American railroads provided a rather interesting train service for mail and express, which also included milk shipments and in some cases LCL (Less than Carload Lot) shipments. Most of the intercity train consists included a Rail Post Office. The RPO could either be a complete car providing 60 feet of postal sorting space, or it could be a combination RPO-baggage/express with either 30 feet or 15 feet devoted to the postal operations. Later on with the new streamlined cars, 85-foot lightweight equipment could be designed with a 60-foot RPO section, and 15 to 20 feet devoted to either checked baggage or express shipments. There were also 60-foot lightweight cars devoted completely to the RPO service. The mail sorting service was provided for the U.S. Postal Service and the Canadian Post Service, and

the cars were marked U.S. Mail Railway Post Office, or sometimes Mail Service in Canada.

Baggage and express cars were designed solely for handling the Railway Express Agency shipments and/or checked baggage. The heavyweight cars varied in length from about 60 feet to over 80 feet, depending upon the design and the car builder. Streamlined baggage and express cars ranged in size from 70 feet to 85 feet.

The standard heavyweight and streamlined mail and express equipment were not the only cars assigned to such service. Many of the railroads converted, or ordered directly as new, express boxcars that were 40 to 50 feet long depending upon the design. The cars were equipped with steam lines and could be operated with the other equipment. Both the railroad lines and the Railway Express Agency owned the equipment with their own lettering and color schemes.

The RPO and baggage/express cars were commonly known as "head-end" cars as they were generally situated between the motive power and the passenger carrying equipment. However, it was not uncommon to find such equipment on the rear of a passenger train. This was a common operation when the cars were to be set out while en route, and other equipment was to be picked up.

One of the interesting aspects of the mail and express service was the dedicated trains for such operations. They were often referred to as the Fast Mail. Many of the railroads operated such trains, such as the Great Northern, Milwaukee Road, Santa Fe, New York Central, Union Pacific, and the list can continue.

The Fast Mail trains varied in length from as short as six to eight cars to well over twenty. Some mail trains, such as the Milwaukee Road's Fast Mail between Chicago and St. Paul-Minneapolis had as many as four Rail Post Office cars. Most of the trains operated with one car with a 60-foot RPO section, or two cars with 30-foot sections that were coupled together. In many cases, the Fast Mail trains were totally devoted to the mail and express traffic with a mixture of streamlined, heavyweight and box express cars. And by the way, Express Refrigerator cars were also operated for perishable food products. Most of the latter equipment was owned and operated by Railway Express, later known as the REA.

Speaking of the Fast Mail trains, they either operated as devoted trains or included a coach for passenger service. One example was the Milwaukee Road's Fast Mail between Chicago and the Twin Cities. The westbound train did not include any coach service while the eastbound operation had one coach. The Great Northern's Fast Mail between St. Paul and Seattle also operated with one coach. Much of the Milwaukee Road's Fast Mail consist was interchanged with the Great Northern in St. Paul for the remainder of the trip to the West Coast.

The mail trains also had numerous cars from many other railroads. For example, one could observe Milwaukee Road, Erie, New York Central, and Pennsylvania head-end equipment in the consist of the GN's Fast Mail. The mixture of head-end equipment was also true of the other passenger trains. For example, the Chicago and North Western's Ashland Limited between Chicago and Ashland, Wisconsin, often included a Great Northern baggage car. Thus model railroaders have an opportunity to have a mixed railroad consist in their passenger operations, either as a full mail and express, or a regular passenger train which could have anywhere from one to six or seven head-end cars behind the motive power, and anywhere from one to six cars on the rear-end. These numbers of course could vary with service requirements and volume for each day of the week.

The following photos illustrate some of the type of mail and express service and the variety of train consists and equipment for the MAIL AND EXPRESS traffic on the North American Railroads.

Still another important traffic on many of the overnight passenger trains was milk transport. The milk was secure in milk cans as can be observed in this photo. The cans were loaded into baggage cars and delivered to various points along the way. This is one of the reasons many overnight trains were referred to as "Milk Trains." The milk traffic in this photo is being unloaded at Denver, Colorado, in 1969. The trains were often very conveniently scheduled for the milk transport to arrive at destinations rather early. *Herman Page*

The Boston and Maine provided extensive mail and express service between Boston and Troy, New York, a distance of 190.4 miles. This photo illustrates a train at Troy with a mixture of head-end equipment, such as Refrigerator Express cars (the first car) and a mixture of baggage cars for express and baggage plus the Rail Post Office for mail services. The B&M 4-8-2, No. 4117, is smoking it up as it moves through Troy in July 1946. *Harold K. Vollrath Collection*

Mail trains operated not only in overnight services, but also over longer distances, such as this Santa Fe transcontinental mail train. This train, No. 8, is eastbound near Kingman, Arizona, with a ten-car consist including a combine as the rear car for the train crew. The consist includes two Box Express cars, one 60-foot Rail Post Office car, and six baggage cars for both express and mail. *June 1967, Herman Page*

Head-end cars for mail and express came in all shapes and sizes. This particular car may have been out of service when photographed in Lafayette, Louisiana, in 1946. The car was originally a Rail Post Office car and appears to be less than 50 feet long. The name in the letter board is Southern Pacific, and the car was a Texas and New Orleans Railroad car with the number T&NO 250. Note the smaller door which was common for the RPO section of the car. However, the RPO lettering has been removed and replaced with the word "Baggage" to the left of the door on the right, and the words "Railway Express Agency" to the right of the same door. This is just one example of the different varieties of head-end cars in service before Amtrak. *Harold K. Vollrath Collection*

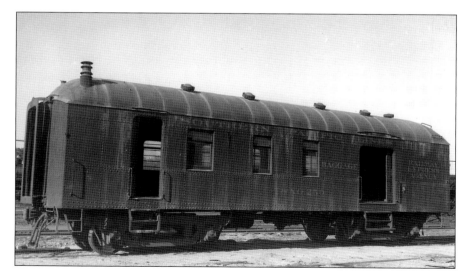

Boston and Maine Baggage Car No.3298 is a typical example of the heavyweight baggage cars built for baggage, express and storage or bulk mail service. The Boston and Maine lettering was not in the letter board as was typical of most passenger equipment. It is fading out but is located between the doors in the center of the car. *Boston, Mass., 1953, Harold K. Vollrath Collection*

Here is a lightweight streamlined Southern Pacific baggage car, No. 6730. The lettering is fading out as the car was in service for Amtrak when photographed in 1972 in the Twin Cities (St. Paul-Minneapolis). *Patrick C. Dorin*

Atlantic Coast Line stream-lined Rail Post Office car No. 7 is approximately 60 feet long and has a full 60-foot interior for the postal service. Several railroads owned and operated such equipment, such as the Santa Fe and The Milwaukee Road. The car's portrait was taken in service during a station stop at Augusta, Georgia, in February 1966. Note the swinging arm on the door of the car, which was used to pick-up mailbags without stopping at many stations along the route. *Harold K. Vollrath Collection*

Many head-end cars were combination mail and express, otherwise known as Rail Post Office-baggage cars. This photo shows a Louisiana and Arkansas car No. 3 with a 30-foot RPO section and two doors for express, baggage and extra bulk mail. The lettering on the car illustrates the RPO section and the Railway Express Agency section. Note the Kansas City Southern Lines in the letter board with the L&A No. 3, indicating the car is own by the Louisiana and Arkansas, a subsidiary of the KCS. Photographed at New Orleans in March 1957. *Harold K. Vollrath Collection*

This Illinois Central RPO-baggage is an 85-foot light streamlined car with a 60-foot RPO section. It is also lettered for the Railway Express Agency and Baggage. Photographed at Homewood, Illinois, in the mid-1960s. A streamlined baggage car is illustrated to the right of the RPO-baggage, and is equipped with six-wheel trucks. *Patrick C. Dorin*

This streamlined Illinois Central car is a combination baggage-coach. Note the lettering "Baggage" to the left of the car. It had been awhile since the car had been washed, and therefore the number was not visible. However, it is No. 1850 and was assigned to the head-end of the Governor's Special, an IC train between Chicago and Springfield in early 1971 — just prior to Amtrak. The 81-foot car rode on six wheel trucks and was equipped with a 29-foot baggage section plus seating for 36 coach passengers. *Patrick C. Dorin*

This Minneapolis and St. Louis Railroad gas-electric No. GE29 was a combination Rail Post Office (30 foot section) - baggage car and provided the power for local service on the railroad. In this photo it is not in passenger service but rather providing the power for an M&StL business car as shown to the right. *Harold K. Vollrath Collection*

Southern Pacific's train numbers 19 and 20 provided the mail service between Portland and the San Francisco Bay area. No. 19 is pausing here at Davis, California, en route to the Bay area. *W. C. Whittaker*

The C&NW trains between Duluth/Superior and Chicago were the primary mail carriers for decades until the late 1950s. At that time, the C&NW gave up the mail traffic and eventually discontinued all overnight train service between Duluth and Chicago. An RPO is being loaded with mail at Cameron, Wisconsin, which is located between Superior and Eau Claire. The Rail Post Office service, if it were to be put back in operation, would eliminate the back haulage of mail to and from hubs. That in turn would save on fuel costs, and is one more example of how the railroad industry can bring about a more economical system of transportation. Many would probably not agree with the idea for mail haulage. *The Lake Superior Railroad Museum Collection*

The Milwaukee Road had the primary mail contract between the Twin Cities and Chicago — and the Great Northern between the Twin Cities and Seattle. The Fast Mail was the name of the trains on the GN and Milwaukee Road. The Milwaukee Road also operated a day train from Minneapolis to Chicago, train No. 58, which also handled a substantial amount of mail and express traffic. No. 58 is shown here at La Crosse, Wisconsin, with three units for power and a consist of over 15 cars. *Lloyd Keyser*

The Penn Central merger brought about combinations of New York Central and Pennsylvania motive power on the passenger trains. This particular train is pausing at Toledo, Ohio, in 1968, and express is being loaded and unloaded at the station. *Bob Lorenz*

SP train No. 54 was a connection with the San Joaquin Daylight at Lathrop for passengers and express traffic between Sacramento and Los Angeles. The short one-car train with a streamlined combine was called the Sacramento Daylight. *Patrick C. Dorin Collection*

The Missouri Pacific's Texas Eagle, train No. 122, is getting ready to roll at Houston, Texas. To the right and left of the photo, there are baggage-express cars for both loading and unloading both Railway Express shipments and the U.S. Mail. The Houston Union Station building is in the background in this photo taken on February 17, 1961. *William Raia*

This Seaboard Air Line train at Hialeah, Florida, illustrates the usual make-up of equipment for mail and express at the head-end of the train. The consist includes two baggage cars, one REA Express box car, and one REA Express refrigerator car, plus a mixture of heavyweight and streamlined coaches, sleeping cars and food and beverage equipment. Although it is not certain, this could be the consist of the Palmland, a New York – Miami, which provided service for many communities along the route. The train departed New York and Miami in the late evening, with an early arrival the second morning at the destination. The Palmland could be classified as an all-purpose train, which is shown here at the Hialeah, Florida, yard, just three-plus miles north of Miami. *William Raia*

The Denali Star is departing Fairbanks for Anchorage in this July 2000 view. The first car behind the motive power is a baggage-power car (for head-end power for the passenger equipment), and the second car is a dome coach. The Denali Star has new and/or rebuilt passenger equipment, which resembles the passenger equipment in operation in the U.S. and Canada for decades. *Patrick C. Dorin*

CHAPTER 9

THE ALASKA RAILROAD

The Alaska Railroad is known as the only "Full Service Railroad" in the United States. The company operates passenger services north to Fairbanks as well as to Seward and Whittier. The train to Fairbanks is known as the Denali Star, the train to Seward is the Coastal Classic while the service to Whittier is Glacier Discovery.

The trains are equipped with new coaches and dining cars built by Daewod Hesug Industries. This equipment was built to the same measurements as the passenger equipment that has been around for decades. The Alaska Railroad has coaches and dining cars from the Union Pacific, and also dome coaches that once operated on both the UP and the Northern Pacific.

All of the trains include a baggage-power car for the electrical heating, lighting, and air-conditioning systems. The make-up of the trains includes the coaches (and a dome coach) and a dining car. The trains also have various tour groups with several passenger cars attached to the rear. The Denali Star operates with as many as 20 cars or more including the tour group equipment.

The following photos illustrate part of the Alaska Railroad passenger-car fleet and the Denali Star.

This baggage-power car allows the railroad to operate any type of motive power without head-end power on the passenger trains. Note the rear of the motive power just ahead of the baggage-power car, which is part of the consist of the Denali Star. *Patrick C. Dorin*

Coach 209 is part of the new fleet of coach equipment built in Korea during the 1990s. The new equipment is basically the same size as the streamlined coaches that operated on the railroads for decades. That is, in the 85-feet-long category as well as the same height to the top of the car, which matches the rebuilt dome cars from either the Union Pacific or the Northern Pacific. *Patrick C. Dorin*

The coach seating arrangement on the new Alaska Railroad coaches. *Patrick C. Dorin*

Dining Car No. 401 in the consist of the Denali Star. *Patrick C. Dorin*

The interior of the new dining cars on the Alaska Railroad is similar to the dining room areas found on many types of dining cars over the decades. *Patrick C. Dorin*

The dome coach No. 521 is a former Northern Pacific car. The Alaska Railroad also acquired dome cars from the Union Pacific. *Patrick C. Dorin*

Interior of the dome of Car No. 502, which is a former Union Pacific car. *Patrick C. Dorin*

Coaches were equipped with overhead baggage racks, which made it very convenient for passengers. Note the luggage on the racks above the windows. The seats could also be rotated so that two folks on each seat could face each other for easy conversation. *Great Northern Railway Photo, Lake Superior Railroad Museum Collection*

CHAPTER 10

A PASSENGER EQUIPMENT REVIEW

The purpose of this chapter is to take a look at examples of passenger equipment operated in North America from the 1940s through to the Amtrak Era. The photos and diagrams include the head-end equipment, such as baggage cars, Rail Post Office cars and combines, coaches, dining and lounge cars, parlor cars, and sleeping cars.

Coach seating for intercity train service was often equipped with deep cushion reclining seats and adjustable footrests. *Great Northern Railway Photo, Lake Superior Railroad Museum Collection*

Many overnight and transcontinental trains were equipped with coaches with leg-rest seating. The lady to the right in the photo is making use of the leg-rest for her relaxation. *Great Northern Railway Photo, Lake Superior Railroad Museum Collection*

Long distance coaches were often equipped with larger restrooms which included a dressing room. This was very convenient for men to shave when getting up, and for women to take care of their make-up needs. *Great Northern Railway Photo, Lake Superior Railroad Museum Collection*

Many passenger trains, such as the Great Northern's Western Star, were equipped with coffee-shop lounge cars for food and beverage service. Such equipment included a lunch counter and table seating for meal and beverage service and a lounge area. *Great Northern Railway Photo, Lake Superior Railroad Museum Collection*

Menu

Dining Car facilities available to Coach Passengers
Full Course meals from $2.50 and up served in Dining Car
Children's menu at reduced prices available in Dining Car

A LA CARTE

SALADS
Grapefruit and Orange 90
Head Lettuce 75
Lettuce and Tomato 90
Served with French Dressing
and Crackers

BREADS
Toast 25
Ry-Krisp 25
Assorted Breads 25

EGGS, MEAT
Eggs—as you like them (2) 55
Sausage, Ham or Bacon and Eggs 1.25
French Fried Potatoes—per serving 35

DESSERTS
Fresh Baked Pie 35
Pie Ala Mode 55
Grapefruit (half) 30
Preserved Pears or Peaches 35
American Cheese and Crackers 45
Ice Cream 25

BEVERAGES
Tea, Pot (hot or iced) 30
Cocoa or Coffee, Pot 30
Milk (Whole, Skim or
Buttermilk) 20
Malted Milk or Milk Shake 40

SANDWICHES

Please specify if desired on toast

Tuna Fish Salad .... .75	Bacon, Lettuce and Tomato .... .85	
American Cheese .... .50	Hamburger .... .60	
Fried Egg .... .50	Cheeseburger .... .75	
Fried Ham .... .75	California Burger .... .85	

Peanut Butter and Jelly 50

Rocky Suggests... for SNACK or LUNCHEON

"Perfect Pickin's"
CHICKEN IN A BASKET
$1.75

Milk fed spring chicken—fried
to perfection—served with gold-
en French fries and tangy cole
slaw.

Hot Roll—Honey Butter

Coffee - Tea (Hot or Iced) - Milk

WAGON WHEEL SPECIAL
HOT SIRLOIN OF BEEF
SANDWICH
$1.50

Tender slices of beef on bread-
covered with rich pan gravy—
served with whipped potatoes,
cole slaw.

Coffee - Tea (Hot or Iced) - Milk

SEAFOOD 'n FRIES
IN A BASKET
$1.95

An assortment of Jumbo Shrimp,
Deep Sea Scallops and fresh
water fish—spicy cocktail sauce
—served with French Fries,
zesty cole slaw.

Hot Roll—Butter

Coffee - Tea (Hot or Iced) - Milk

RANCH BURGER
In A BASKET
$1.35

Grilled pure ground Jumbo beef
pattie on toasted sesame bun,
topped with a slice of American
cheese and creamy cole slaw,
served with golden French
fries, pickle slices.

Coffee - Tea (Hot or Iced) - Milk

No Substitutions, Please.

Employes are not permitted to serve verbal orders

Form 2821-L-D—7-64

This view illustrates the lounge seating area for the Great Northern's Ranch Car, which was a drawing card for passengers to travel again on the GN, which had a very positive attitude toward passenger service. *Great Northern Railway Photo, Lake Superior Railroad Museum Collection*

Full dining cars provided seating at tables for four passengers as well as smaller tables for two passengers. *Great Northern Railway Photo, Lake Superior Railroad Museum Collection*

Sleeping cars provided a variety of accommodations for overnight and longer distance travel. The open section was a budget-priced accommodation with daytime seating, as shown here, and a lower and upper berth. *Great Northern Railway Photo, Lake Superior Railroad Museum Collection*

The open sections provided sleeping comfort with foam-rubber cushioned mattresses. Each berth, upper and lower, had individual reading lights, a shelf or hammock for sundry items, and clothes hangers. The open section concept continued in use well into the streamlined era. This photo shows where the upper and lower berths were located as well as the ladder to reach the upper berth. *Great Northern Railway Photo, Lake Superior Railroad Museum*

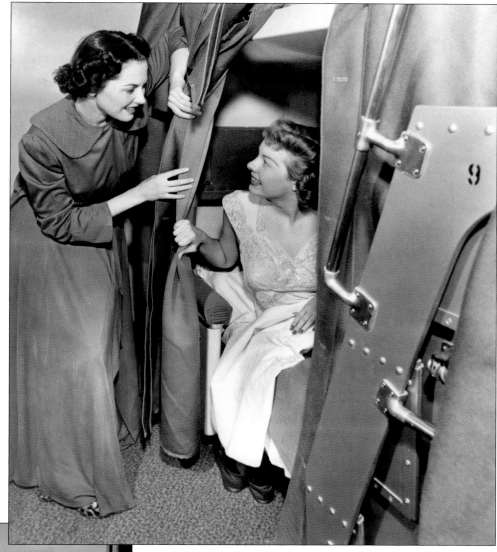

The roomette was a private room accommodation for one passenger, which included a small toilet and folding sink in the small room. This photo illustrates the roomette with the bed made up, which incidentally folded down from the wall. *Great Northern Railway Photo, Lake Superior Railroad Museum Collection*

This is a top down photo of a roomette with its single seat, the small toilet at the front of the lady's feet and folding sink above, as well as other features such as clothing hooks and mirror. Switches on a convenient control panel enabled passengers to regulate temperature, ventilation and lighting. The seating had a sponge rubber back and seat cushions with folding armrests. Ceiling and reading lights provided appropriate illumination. The roomettes allowed for complete privacy. *Great Northern Railway Photo, Lake Superior Railroad Museum Collection*

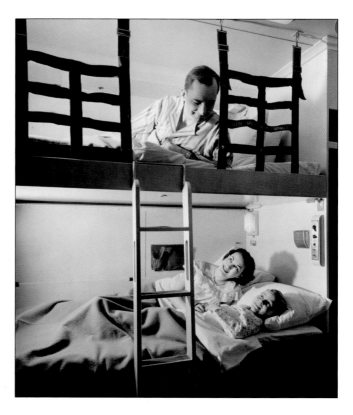

The double bedroom included a full sofa for daytime travel plus each room had its own private toilet facilities. Temperature, lighting and ventilation could be controlled by the passenger(s). Each bedroom provided both upper and lower berth and were very convenient for family travel. Partitions which separated adjoining bedrooms could be opened to create one large room for families or other groups traveling together. *Great Northern Railway Photo, Lake Superior Railroad Museum Collection*

Full lounge cars were operated on many of the longer distance trains, both day and night as well as transcontinental services. Lounge cars provided seating for relaxation, seating at tables for playing cards, enjoying refreshments and having a chance to meet and make new friends. The lounge cars, in many cases, had a small desk for passengers to use for writing letters and taking notes about the superb train trip. This view shows the interior of the observation lounge car operated on the Western Star by the Great Northern. *Great Northern Railway Photo, Lake Superior Railroad Museum Collection*

Parlor cars were operated on many intercity trains. The accommodations were single rotating reclining seats as illustrated here in the interior of a former Great Northern Dining-Parlor Car, No. 1060. Note the dining room to the rear of the photo. *Great Northern Railway Photo*

For a final look at interiors, we have a photo from the Pullman Company dating back to the early 1900s. The type of coach seat in this view was once common for day coaches and without reclining seating. However, the type of seat shown here is also common for various types of commuter passenger equipment with flip-over backs in the many cars constructed since the 1970s. *Patrick C. Dorin Collection*

Baggage and express cars were designed to match the passenger-carrying equipment, such as this streamlined Southern Pacific baggage-express car. This equipment was also classified as a mail storage car, depending upon the different designs and the specific railroad company. *Patrick C. Dorin*

This Rail Post Office-baggage car was equipped with a 30-foot mail sorting section while the remainder of the car had two sets of doors on each side designed for Railway Express and passenger baggage. Chesapeake and Ohio car No. 89 is part of the consist of train No. 11 at Grand Rapids, Michigan, in July 1969. *Patrick C. Dorin*

An example of a streamlined RPO-baggage is the Great Northern No. 1107, shown here as part of the Badger's consist at Duluth, Minnesota, in 1967. *Patrick C. Dorin*

The most common combination car was the baggage-coach. Such equipment was operated on all types of trains including mixed trains. As mentioned earlier, the mixed train was the last type of passenger service on many branches — a freight train with a car for passengers and express, and sometimes even mail service. Great Northern No. 566 was operated on mixed trains. This photo was taken at Great Falls, Montana, in August 1949, and is on the rear of a freight train. *William C. Whittaker*

The Duluth, Missabe and Iron Range Coach No. 33 is an example of a heavyweight coach. The car is shown here in a special train with Burlington Northern streamlined passenger equipment at Duluth, Minnesota. The 33 was built in 1919 and is still in regular operation in 2008 on the North Shore Scenic Railroad, which operates between Duluth and Two Harbors. *Patrick C. Dorin*

Railroads often sold their passenger equipment to other railroad companies, and later even to museums. This Great Northern streamlined coach, No. 1078 in the Big-Sky Blue color scheme — the last colors of the GN — was purchased from the Chicago and North Western during the 1960s. The car operated in the C&NW 400 fleet of streamliners. *Patrick C. Dorin*

The "Dome Car," where one could look up, down and all around, was one of the neatest ways for travel and seeing the country. Dome cars were operated on most of the primary long distance trains between Chicago and the West Coast, and also between Chicago and Florida, and between Chicago and Washington, D.C. Dome cars were built as coaches, sleeping cars, lounge cars and dining cars. This particular car was the former Northern Pacific Coach No. 555, which became Burlington Northern 555. The cars operated on the North Coast Limited, and later with the event of Amtrak, the fleet of former GN and NP cars operated on the Empire Builder and what became known as the North Coast Hiawatha. The car is shown here in the consist of an early Amtrak train arriving in Chicago in the summer of 1971.

The Missouri Pacific was a positive passenger train promoter, and ordered high quality equipment from builders such as American Car and Foundry and the Budd Company. The MP's 850 was designated a Delux Coach and was built in September 1948. *ACF Photo, Patrick C. Dorin Collection*

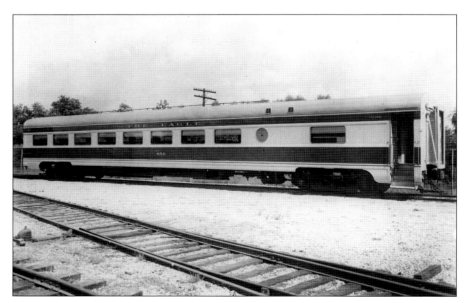

This photo of the C&NW's Dining Car No. 6917 was painted the UP's two-tone grey color scheme for operation on the Overland in the mid-1940s. This view illustrates the picture windows for the dining room to the left, and for the hallway side to the right. *Jeff M. Koeller Collection*

It was 1939 when the C&NW Diner No. 6934's portrait was taken in Berkeley, California. This view shows the kitchen side of the car plus the pair windows for the dining room. The car is lettered for the Treasure Island Special. *W. C. Whittaker*

Great Northern's rebuilt dining car, the Minnesota, is an example of a streamlined car and is shown here in extra service on the rear of the Badger at Superior, Wisconsin, in the mid-1960s. *Patrick C. Dorin*

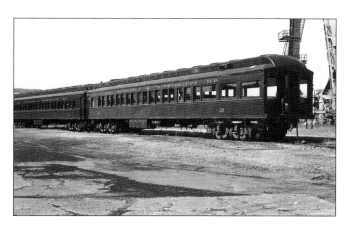

One example of a streamlined lightweight sleeping car is the Great Northern "Harrison Glacier." This was a 16 duplex roomette, 4 double bedroom car assigned to the Empire Builder, as one can observe with the lettering on the car. *Pullman-Standard Photo, Patrick C. Dorin Collection*

The Duluth, Missabe and Iron Range Railway operated Solarium coaches on their trains between Duluth and the Mesabi Range (Hibbing and Virginia, Minnesota) and Duluth and Ely. The cars were paired window cars with larger and end windows in the observation section. DM&IR's No. 29 went to the Lake Superior and Mississippi Railroad, a tourist line operating during summer weekends in west Duluth. The LS&M travels over a segment of the former Northern Pacific, which by the way at one time operated commuter trains to the far western end of Duluth, a community known as Fond du Lac. *Patrick C. Dorin*

Heavyweight sleeping cars rode on six-wheel trucks and were operated by the Pullman Company for many decades. For the most part, the cars were painted in the Pullman Green colors. As the streamlined era progressed, many of the Standard Heavyweight sleepers and coaches were repainted in the new colors. In many instances, the railroad name was in the letter board, while the words "Pullman" were sub-lettering in the upper corners. Modelers, by the way, have many opportunities to model such equipment, such as the Walthers Heavyweight Southern Pacific sleeper, the Sunburst Rose shown here. *Dan Mackey*

Most observation cars were combination cars, such as parlor observations or sleeping car observations. This illustration shows train No. 19, the Gopher departing Duluth for St. Paul with the parlor observation car, No. 1083, the Twin Cities. These cars were rebuilt from heavyweight parlor cars and were assigned to the Badger and Gopher between Duluth-Superior and the Twin Cities. *Patrick C. Dorin*

Some of the most dramatic observation-sleeping cars were the Sky-tops operated on the Milwaukee Road's Olympian Hiawatha between Chicago and Seattle-Tacoma. When the Olympian Hi was discontinued, the Canadian National purchased part of the fleet and repainted the cars in the CN's black and light grey scheme. The Gaspe is shown here on the rear of the Ocean. The CN operated the cars on the Ocean and the Scotian between Montreal and Halifax during the mid to late 1960s. They later were assigned to a variety of other trains. *Jim Scribbins*

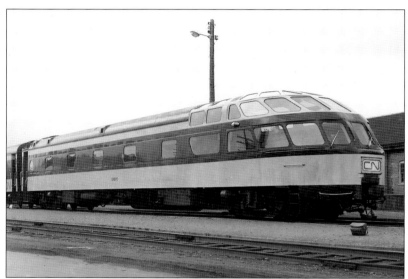

Streamlined observation cars came in a variety of designs with either the rounded end, such as the C&NW parlor-observation car bringing up the rear of the Twin Cities 400, or square ends such as the Great Northern previously illustrated. Several dome observation cars were built for the Burlington's Zephyr fleet. The 400 is shown here at Sussex, Wisconsin. *Mark Llanuza*

This photo illustrates two types of observation cars. One is the open end, which was once common for heavyweight sleeping cars. In this case, the car is a C&O business car on the rear of the Sportsman. To the upper right, one can observe a New York Central sleeper observation car. This portrait was taken in August 1966 at the Toledo, Ohio, Union Station. *Bob Lorenz*

Railroad company business cars were operated for inspection trips, meetings, and for shippers. Most often the equipment operated on the rear of a regular passenger train, and even on freight trains. The BN's Mississippi River was a former Burlington car, while the Yellowstone River was a former Northern Pacific. The car located ahead of the Mississippi River was the parlor car that once operated on the Great Northern's Gopher between the Twin Cities and Duluth-Superior. The Yellowstone River is attached to the rear of an Amtrak train. The business cars were equipped with two or four bedrooms, depending upon design, a dining room and kitchen and a lounge section at the rear of the car with the open end. *Patrick C. Dorin*

This photo of the Missouri-Kansas-Texas Railroad's Katy Flyer in 1942 provides a good example of passenger equipment and consists. The heavyweight Pullman sleeping car carrying the markers is a 12 section, 1 drawing room car. The next car is a full dining car, which was generally placed between the coaches and sleepers. (But not always) There are two heavyweight coaches in the consist plus four head-end cars, one of which is an RPO-baggage with a 30 foot Rail Post Office section. This steam-powered train in 1942 at Oswego, Missouri, was typical of the types of equipment and consists of overnight trains during the 1930s and '40s. The reader may wish to compare this photo with the Walther's HO gauge Pullman car, the Sunburst Rose previously illustrated in this chapter. *William A. Raia*

The Toronto, Hamilton and Buffalo's 4-6-4, Hudson, No.501, was built in 1930. The 501 is leading 12 cars at 70 miles per hour. Note the two express refrigerator cars on the head end. *Harold K. Vollrath Collection*

CHAPTER 11

A MOTIVE POWER REVIEW

The purpose of this chapter is to take a look at some of the different types of locomotive power for passenger service. There were many types of locomotives built including steam, diesel and electric power. Many of the locomotives assigned to passenger service could easily operate at 75 miles per hour. In fact, there were many types of steam power that could achieve over 110 miles per hour, and a number of passenger diesel power were designed for 117 miles per hour. Indeed, the 1500 horsepower "F" units, built by Electro-Motive Division of General Motors, were able to achieve 120 miles per hour on such railroad lines as the Santa Fe Railway. This ability, of course, would have to do with the type of gearing the mo-

tive power contained. But nevertheless, we talk about high speed train service in the 2000s, when in many cases, the capability was there with the motive power built in the 1940s and '50s for diesel power, and back to the 1920s for steam power.

The following photos are a brief review of the passenger power in operation since the 1920s for steam, and the 1930s for diesel power until Amtrak and beyond. Many of the individual railroad line locomotives powered Amtrak trains for several years after the start-up in May 1971.

Another example of a heavy duty, high-speed steam locomotive is the Burlington's 5634, a 4-8-2 Mountain. The 5634 is shown here at St. Paul, Minnesota, with what appears to be the North Coast Limited. *Harold K. Vollrath Collection*

Electro-Motive Division constructed what began as freight diesel power in the first designs of the "F" units, but was redesigned to include a steam generator (for heating and air-conditioning) for passenger service. EMD constructed several varieties of F units ranging from F-2s to F-9s. The F-9 was a 1750 horsepower, while the F units in this photo, an A and a B, each contain 1500 horsepower. These two Great Northern F units are leading the Dakotan with a heavy consist into the St. Paul Union Station. The units were capable of handling the trains at speeds up to 79 miles per hour, the high speed limit in the GN's Automatic Block Signal Territory. *Great Northern Railway Photo*

EMD also built F units that were four feet longer, and were known as FP units. But that was not all, EMD built these FL-9 units for passenger service on the New Haven. The FL-9s were equipped with two-axle trucks at the front, and three-axle trucks at the rear. The units were built to operate either with the diesel power, or on electric power from a third rail operating into New York City. This train is at East Hartford in the New York City – Boston corridor. *Bob Lorenz Collection*

For still another motive power design for both freight and passenger service, besides the F units previously illustrated, EMD developed the GP units, meaning General Purpose. The Great Northern's 602 is a GP-7 with 1500 horsepower. The long hood was the front on the GN Geeps, as these units were called. One advantage of the GP style is that the locomotive did not need to be turned at the end of a branch line or for commuter train service for the return trip. Many train services were able to use the passenger geeps with this advantage. Just one example was the Pennsylvania Railroad commuter train operations between Chicago and Valparaiso. The units were simply switched to the opposite end of the train. Furthermore, during the layover between runs, the GP type of power could and was used for switching or handling a freight train. *Great Northern Railway Photo*

Another example of a GP operated in passenger service is the Illinois Central power assigned to the "Governor's Special" between Chicago and Springfield, Illinois. The 9201 is shown here departing Homewood en route to Springfield. The 9201 is a GP-9 with 1750 horsepower. *Patrick C. Dorin*

The Great Northern also had a small fleet of NW-3s, 1000 horsepower, basically a lengthened switch engine with a steam generator located ahead of the cab. These engines were often assigned to two-car passenger trains in service on branch lines. In this case, GN 181 is handling a mixed train (freight and passenger) from Grand Forks, North Dakota, to a branch line leading to Hannah, North Dakota, a distance of 125 miles. The train made a round trip on a daily except Sunday basis. *Great Northern Railway Photo*

The Great Northern also invested in EMD's E-7 passenger units with 2000 horsepower. The 506 is shown here along with a passenger GP-9 (the 670 in the new GN Sky Blue paint scheme) heading up train No. 19, the Gopher soon to depart for Minneapolis and St. Paul. The train is at the Duluth Union Station, which now houses the Lake Superior Railroad Museum and the North Shore Scenic Railroad station facilities. The NSSR operates trains between Duluth and Two Harbors. The Gopher ran on a 3 hour, 15 minute schedule for the 160 miles between Duluth and St. Paul. *Patrick C. Dorin*

EMD also produced the E units in both A and B unit configurations; the A units had a cab, while the B units were without a cab. The Missouri Pacific 7003 is an EMD E-6 with 2000 horsepower. The A unit heads up a B unit leading the Colorado Eagle at Denver, Colorado. The MP design had portholes instead of rectangular windows. *Photo by D. Christiansen, William A. Raia Collection*

The Missouri Pacific also invested in the Alco-GE PAs for passenger power with 2000 horsepower. The 8023 is shown here at Denver in 1956. *Photo by D. Christensen, William A. Raia Collection*

The top of the line of passenger motive power came in the form of E-8s and E-9s, 2250 horsepower and 2400 horsepower respectively. The 4034 and 2021 are back to back. The 4034 was an E-9 with 2400 horsepower. The two units are leading the City of New Orleans at Homewood, Illinois, in the late 1960s. *Patrick C. Dorin*

C&NW's E unit, No. 5024A, was refitted with head-end power, (a Cummins engine) which replaced the steam generator. The new bi-level equipment for the Flambeau 400 and the Peninsula 400, and the new bi-level gallery commuter passenger equipment relied on electrical power (instead of steam) from the HEP for lighting, heating and air-conditioning. Steam generators were incorporated into the new diesel power at the beginning since all of the passenger equipment was designed for steam generation for heating and air-conditioning. Since the late 1980s, virtually all passenger power in operation utilizes the HEP concept. *Thomas Dorin Collection*

EPILOGUE

THE SUNSET OF TRAIN SERVICE / THE SUNRISE OF AMTRAK

The 1960s saw sharp declines in passenger train services throughout North America. There was less and less patronage, except in some cases with commuter train services and some isolated train services. One example is the Algoma Central out of Sault Ste. Marie, Ontario. By 1970, train services and schedules were a skeleton of what they were even in 1950. Not only were passenger trains being discontinued, but railroad routes were also being abandoned and torn up.

Amtrak was designed and went into operation in May 1971. Rumor has it that Amtrak was created to set up a plan to discontinue all passenger rail services. But that was not going to happen. Slowly but surely, patronage began to grow because of congestion and many other travel problems. Moving ahead to the 21st century, Amtrak patronage is at record levels and growing. Plus, with the new services created in California, that state now has more passenger trains than ever. The only area lacking service is northern California. However, from Sacramento to San Diego, the train service has been the rising star.

Looking at the Northeast corridor, we also see substantial increases in the number of passenger trains. The transcontinental services are carrying record number of passengers too. Many of the corridor services, such as Chicago – Milwaukee are skyrocketing.

North America, with Amtrak, VIA Rail Canada, and the many new commuter rail authorities and railroads, is truly on the verge of a new and bright SUNRISE in public transportation. Yes, North America, it is best to STAY ON TRACK. This would mean coordinated services with both bus and air services. It is refreshing to know that many areas now have the convenience of an all-weather transportation with the greatest potential for travel safety.

The beginning of Amtrak's passenger train consists were often a mixture of various railroad companies' equipment and colors. Even the new mergers found the new road names mixed with the names of the previous companies, such as the Burlington Northern and Northern Pacific in this photo at the Milwaukee Station around late 1971 *Jim Scribbins*

It was not uncommon for Amtrak power to be mixed with individual railroad locomotives, such as Amtrak's 110 and the Southern Pacific's 6455. Note the rigging on top of the power set up to knock off ice at tunnel entrances to avoid breaking the dome-car windows. *Stockton, California, May 1975, Harold K. Vollrath Collection*

Eventually a number of Amtrak trains were reequipped with the Metroliner design coaches and café cars. This six-car train is en route from the Twin Cities to Duluth, Minnesota, on the Burlington Northern's former Great Northern line. *Patrick C. Dorin*

The Duluth train was eventually converted to an overnight between Duluth and Chicago via the Twin Cities. The North Star is at the Midway Station stop (St. Paul-Minneapolis) while en route to Chicago. The consist included coaches, meal and beverage service and sleeping car service. The trains have been gone since 1985, and there are plans (although all too slow) to reestablish train service between Duluth and Minneapolis. Possibly, the trains would arrive at Minneapolis for an over-the-platform transfer to the Hiawatha Light Rail System. (That is part of the plan, which is under construction for the new commuter rail service — the North Star line between Minneapolis and Big Lake, Minnesota.
Patrick C. Dorin

Frank Schnick has caught on film two examples of Amtrak train services between Chicago and New York and Washington, D.C. These eastbound trains are rolling through Chesterton, Indiana, in 1992, and are equipped with passenger cars from the mid-1950s. And by the way, there is a lot to learn from that type of equipment, and perhaps the designs could be used for new passenger equipment in the 21st century. After all, that is part of what the Alaska Railroad did.

Although the intercity services in the United States and Canada are provided by Amtrak and VIA Rail Canada, one can still observe and ride passenger trains with motive power and equipment from the days before Amtrak in 1971. The Canadian Pacific has operated a number of steam powered special trains on the Soo Line routes as well as in Canada. *Mark Llanuza*

The Elgin, Joliet and Eastern has been a "Freight Only" railroad for most of its historical existence. However, it has operated many passenger train specials for employees, commuter test trains and for other activities. Here is a ten-car train powered by two EJ&E SD-38-2s and one Amtrak P42 on the double-track line east of Joliet, Illinois. *Mark Llanuza*

Business car trains on the Chicago and North Western, such as this five-car train, including a former Milwaukee Road Super Dome, bring back the memories of the C&NW trains in the bright yellow and green scheme with black striping. *Mark Llanuza*

The C&NW commuter trains retained their color scheme for many of the cars well into the 1970s and beyond when it converted over to the RTA and the Metra Commuter Rail System for the Chicago area. One of the trains is shown here laying overnight at the Richmond Station on the Northwest Line. *Mark Llanuza*

Some C&NW business car trains in the 1990s and beyond were as short as two cars as shown in this photo near Hustler, Wisconsin. *Mark Llanuza*

Business car consists were also attached to the rear of freight trains. This is still a common practice on many rail lines. *Mark Llanuza*

Special passenger trains with freight railroad color schemes operate for many reasons. One example was the Santa Trains at the Christmas Season on the Illinois Central. *Mark Llanuza*

There is one Rail Diesel Car from the 1950s in operation in northern Minnesota. The North Shore Scenic Railroad operates an RDC-1 for tour train service between Duluth and Two Harbors. This illustrates a bit of history from the 1940s through Amtrak. The NSSR No. 9169 is shown here at Two Harbors in August 2007. This car was also used in a test operation for providing commuter train service to Duluth, but not many steps have been taken to achieve this objective despite the high fuel prices as we move through the first decade of the 21st century. *Patrick C. Dorin*

We will finish the photo coverage of different passenger trains since the beginning of Amtrak with a Southern Pacific business car on the rear of Amtrak's Coast Starlight. The train is en route to Portland and has a 19-car consist, which was photographed at Eugene, Oregon. *Patrick C. Dorin*

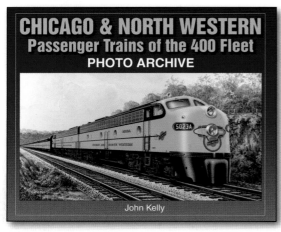
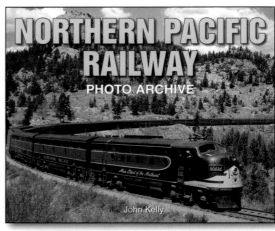
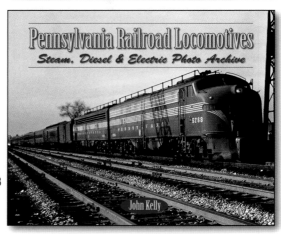

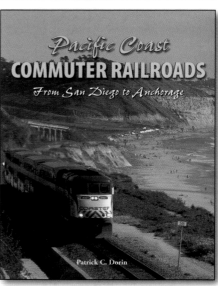
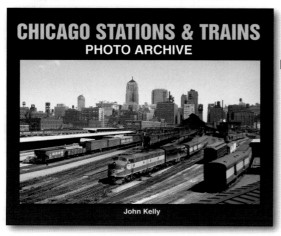